Employees of the Summe Dairy, circa 1928.

The Kresge dime store lunch counter, in 1951.

Star Magazine Presents:

The Best of Remember When

100 Warm Tales of Life As We Lived It

Merry Christmas, Mary Lee —
Lots of our memories
in this book — enjoy!
Love,
Evie & Al
12-25-01

✳ KANSAS CITY STAR BOOKS

Editor: Ronda Cornelius
Design: Jeff Langdon
Artwork: Lisa Morgan

Published by KANSAS CITY STAR BOOKS
1729 Grand Boulevard., Kansas City, Missouri, USA 64108

First edition
Library of Congress Card Number: 2001096174
ISBN: 0-9712920-5-1

Printed in the United States of America
by Walsworth Publishing Co., Marceline, Missouri

Requests for permission to make copies of any part of the
work should be mailed to StarInfo, c/o The Kansas City Star,
1729 Grand Blvd., Kansas City, MO 64108. To order
additional copies, call StarInfo (816) 234-4636 and say
"Operator." Or visit our Web site at www.kcstarinfo.com

Table of Contents

Dancing at the Pla-Mor in the 1940s.

Introduction

On Aug. 15, 1993, Star Magazine announced the debut of a nostalgia column called The Way We Were (renamed Remember When on Jan. 5, 1997). "We need your help," the notice pleaded.

Two weeks later, the first reader-written column began: "I never fully appreciated how nearly perfect my boyhood summers were until I had grown up." That thought resonated with other readers, who have since flooded the Star offices with their own nearly perfect — or at least vivid — memories of growing up and starting out, mostly in the Kansas City area.

Many also wrote about that monumental whirlwind trip to the big city to visit the zoo, the Nelson, the stockyards, the Plaza, Petticoat Lane, Fairyland Park, AND eat at the Forum Cafeteria.

Having to choose just 100 of the more than 350 columns in the archives was reminiscent of the Forum Cafeteria stories: Everything looks so good (even the lime Jell-O), and the tray just gets heavier and heavier.

But, to make the final cut, columns had to have an interesting story, a local angle or universal appeal (that first bike, that junk car), and there had to be a great photo possibility or other art for accompaniment.

A note about the photos: Even with vast local photo archives, it was often impossible to find an exact match, era to subject. Maybe those photos exist in personal family albums or a box in an attic somewhere. But on our limited time frame, we could not go door to door. So, if a photo is off by a few years — or a decade or more — that's why.

Unfortunately, some delectable columns didn't make the tray: how papa repaired the baby's underpants with baling wire before church; how Harold the Rooster terrorized the cats; how an 11-year-old driver smashed the old buggy with the new Ford.

Maybe we'll have to go back for seconds sometime. Until then, keep sending in those memories.

— *Ronda Cornelius, editor*

Herefords in the American Royal arena, circa 1935.

Published on February 20, 2000

American Royal

By Howard James Maddock

I was born on a farm in Bates County, Mo., near Ranch Hill. I went to a one-room school for eight grades, then rode a school bus to town for four grades of high school. Being a farm boy, I naturally took vocational agriculture and was a Future Farmers of America member.

My first visit to Kansas City was when our agriculture teacher chartered a school bus and took us to the American Royal in 1937.

We stayed at the Coates House Hotel at 10th and Broadway. It was an old hotel, but we thought it was grand. It even had an elevator that took us to the third floor, where our rooms were.

We FFA members got into the Royal free by going to the service entrance on Wyoming Street. The main entrance was at the south side on 23rd Street. We could even go into the arena and occupy any empty seats. If all seats were taken for the horse shows in the evening, we could stand in the rear.

Riding the streetcars was fun, but we didn't know our way around very well. We did ride one streetcar that went west from Eighth and Broadway down through a tunnel, then came out of the bluff and went over a tall bridge on its way to the West Bottoms. We had to transfer to another streetcar going south on Genessee Street, then on to Wyoming Street and the American Royal building.

Five of us boys could get a taxi at the hotel and go to the Royal for 25 cents. That was easier and faster.

One night after midnight, a fire truck came up 10th Street with its siren blasting and its red lights flashing. The noise of the siren reverberated between the buildings and was so loud it seemed to be coming right into the hotel. This gave all of us quite a scare.

We were intrigued by all the fine animals on display at the Royal, especially the large draft horses. They had pulling contests between teams of two. The horses were huge, each weighing more than a ton. They don't have this event anymore.

While in Kansas City, we were taken on a tour of the meat-packing industry. We visited Swift, Armour and Cudahay. We saw the complete operation, from slaughter to the finished and packaged products. Kansas City had the second-largest meat processing business in the United States.

We returned home with many good memories of a big city and the American Royal Livestock and Horse Show.

Published on November 21, 1999

American Royal Parade

By Joanne Alton Riordan

Watching the American Royal Parade.

I was 8 and in fourth grade when our family moved to a new house in an area called Leawood, out past the edge of the city and surrounded by open fields. Our house at the north end of High Drive was the 12th to be built in the subdivision. My grade school was a two-room country school, Corinth, about a mile's walk or bike ride down a gravel road from home. With the five new kids from Leawood, there was a total of 40 students at Corinth.

The teachers, Miss Crust and Miss Luthy, each taught four grades and could segue smoothly from first-grade reading to fourth-grade geography or fifth-grade arithmetic to eighth-grade history. They could correct our behavior with just a look or, for serious infractions, a mark on the blackboard indicating a demerit. Five demerits meant we stayed after school — serious consequences!

I believe we all loved going to Corinth. In good weather we played baseball or scrub on a makeshift dirt diamond, with rocks for bases. Foul balls out of left field were temporarily lost in the adjacent cornfield. That wasn't my problem. I was the daydreaming rightfielder. On rainy or snowy days the girls played jacks and the boys played marbles on the floor of the schoolroom, or we roller skated in the basement.

This relaxed atmosphere was quite a contrast to the structure of the big-city school of my earlier years, where there were several rooms for each grade, a cafeteria, a gym and organized games of dodge ball or soccer at recess. I didn't miss any of it.

Two of my classmates rode their horses to school, and one afternoon one of the boys jumped out of the classroom window to retrieve his horse, which had become untethered. The boys were such good riders that they rode in the American Royal Parade each year, and of course we were all on the sidelines waving to them.

The one drawback to our school was its library — a small built-in bookcase. It didn't take long for us to exhaust the available reading material. So when I was 10, my mother decided I was old enough to go to the downtown library. She taught me the order of the streets from the streetcar stop to the library. "Main, Walnut, Grand, McGee, Oak, Locust, Cherry," I'd sing-song.

Corinth grade school is still at 83rd and Mission Road, a sprawling modern building in its fourth incarnation with wonderful playgrounds and a handsome library bulging with books and computers. I know today's students are having great experiences, but I don't think I would trade their years for mine at our two-room school.

The boys were such good riders that they rode in the American Royal Parade each year, and of course we were all on the sidelines waving to them.

Horse riders at the American Royal Parade.

Baltimore Avenue

By Julie Clapp

Looking north on Baltimore Avenue at 11th Street, circa 1950s.

In 1961 I attended a Christmas party at the Hotel Phillips where I met a charming man who introduced himself as Dan Martin. He invited me to dinner the following Saturday. But that evening, as I was dressing, he called to say a business associate had come into town and he had to entertain him. I said I would be happy to join them.

We drove to the Neubern Hotel, and when he emerged with his "associate" I almost laughed out loud. The man was wearing a wide-brimmed fedora, a chalk-striped double-breasted brown suit with lapels out to there, a tattersall vest, a hand-painted yellow tie and brown suede spectator shoes trimmed in alligator. A belted polo coat was draped over his heavily padded shoulders.

As he slid into the back seat I turned to greet him with a smile that quickly faded when I got a good look at his face. Although his mouth was smiling, his eyes were the eyes of a dead man.

Dan started to introduce him and then stopped. "Call me ... Mr. Mann. Yes, that'll do ... Mr. Mann," Dan's associate said with a chuckle.

At Mr. Mann's behest we drove downtown, and the three of us proceeded to visit all the establishments up and down Baltimore Avenue. We went to Gus's, the Famous, the Hotel New Yorker — places I had never set foot in in all my 21 years growing up in Kansas City. They had a faintly raffish reputation and a clientele of lacquered women and cigar-chomping men who were "not our sort of people."

After a few hours of "making the rounds," Mr. Mann decided he was hungry and we made our way to the Sir Loin Room. I was famished, more than slightly tipsy and also annoyed that Mr. Mann and "Danny Boy" (as Mr. Mann called him) had been carrying on a conversation that excluded me. But at dinner Mr. Mann tipped the waiter to have the string quartet play "Indian Love Call," commanding me to join him in a rafter-shaking duet.

Finally he ordered Dan to take him back to the Neubern so that "you two kids can have some fun" — said with a leer that would have made Groucho blush. As he bade me farewell he turned to my date and said, "I like this girl, Danny. She's got class." And with

a tip of his fedora he strode into the hotel.

I had one more date with Dan Martin. When he asked me what I thought he did for a living, I said, "I think you're a gangster." I thought he'd cry. He told me he was in the construction business. He also told me his real name and that he had grown up in Boston as a numbers runner and had been a comic in Las Vegas, but a gangster? Ha ha ha!

Years later I told this story to a fellow who was well acquainted with the ins and outs of KC's criminal element. " '61 was the year the syndicate moved into Kansas City. Don't you remember Appalachia? Mr. Mann was probably a capo sent in to supervise the operation."

What about Dan? "Danny Boy was what they call a 'bag man' — these are the guys who carry money around all over the country."

I've thought about Dan over the years and decided he was a comic in Vegas who gambled and ended up at the mercy of "the boys." Becoming a bag man was the way out.

What a charming, funny, attractive guy. I liked you, Danny, you had class.

They had a faintly raffish reputation and a clientele of lacquered women and cigar-chomping men who were "not our sort of people."

Volker Fountain in 1966.

Published on July 4, 1999

Being cool

By Gretchen Whittaker

You had to be seen several Sundays at Volker Fountain and always be in the middle of the Plaza on Thanksgiving night.

Everyone says, or at least thinks, that life today for a teen-ager is far more stressful than when we grew up. But I remember some fairly stressful times.

In the early 1960s in Prairie Village there were many things you had to know and live by if you were to be able to hold your head up in the late 1960s.

You had to know to have Lee put your school picture up on the board by the cash register downstairs at the Palace. You had to know the best leather purses were at Adler's. You had to know to buy your Madras plaid shirts at Malliard's. You had to know you could sneak a smoke in the ladies bathroom at Jones. You had to take ballroom dancing in the basement of the Toon Shop when you were in seventh grade. And you truly understood stress if you were unlucky enough to have Miss Arth for algebra.

In the second half of the '60s, the stress was unrelenting. You could not be caught riding alone in a back seat. At least once a week-end you had to put in an appearance either at the Vanguard or the Boom Boom Room. You could still sneak a smoke in the Jones bathroom, but the parking lot at Shawnee Mission East was cooler. You had to be seen several Sundays at Volker Fountain and always be in the middle of the Plaza on Thanksgiving night.

You had to know and accept that King's at 75th and Metcalf had the best onion rings, that Winstead's (the only Winstead's) was where you went after a movie, that the Plaza, Brookside and Uptown theaters had the best movies, and that Harzfeld's had great prom dresses. Putsch's Coffee House on the Plaza had the best breakfasts, and Shakey's Pizza on Metcalf had the best

pizza (and your best shot at an illegal brew if you could slip into the "beer side").

By the end of the 1960s there were more rules to follow. You had to lie to your parents about your plans and spend some Saturdays at the Red Dog Inn in Lawrence. Or you had to lie to your parents and go to a "woodsie" and drink beer. Or you had to lie to your parents and skinny-dip in someone's pool. We had a great amount of stress during those years. And we were pretty darn dishonest with our parents. And we thought we were getting away with all of it. And we tried things we were too young for, too old for and too smart for. A foreign war was a vague rumor that increasingly showed up in the news.

Wait — I forget. Am I writing about me in the 1960s or my daughter in the 1990s?

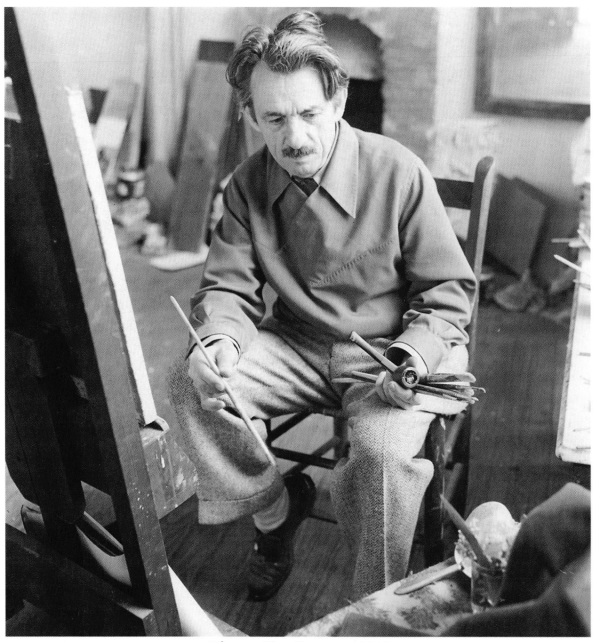

Thomas Hart Benton in 1941.

Published on November 5, 2000

Benton: the artist

By Holland Harpool

Benton's portrait of Lincoln at Lincoln University, in Jefferson City; photo taken in 1955.

To say I was awestruck would be the understatement of the millennium.

When I was a small boy I had two goals in life: to become a famous Broadway actor and an artist whose paintings would hang in galleries the world over. By the time I became a young adult, I was working as a copywriter in an advertising agency, hoping to save enough money to be able to attend classes at the Kansas City Art Institute. I was also acting in plays.

When this particular moment in my life occurred, I was in a play at the University of Missouri-Kansas City. One evening I received an exciting phone call from the play's director, Lowell Matson. He said he had been contacted by Thomas Hart Benton, who was working on a mural for Lincoln University in Jefferson City. The artist was looking for a tall, thin man to pose for the Lincoln figure in the mural. Since I was a little over 6 feet tall and weighed under 140 pounds, Matson thought of me immediately.

A few days later, outfitted in a Lincolnesque costume from the theater's wardrobe department, I found myself standing in Benton's studio. Stacked against the wall were several of his paintings, including "Susanna and the Elders." To say I was awestruck would be the understatement of the millennium.

At the end of our first session, we adjourned to Benton's kitchen, where I shared coffee and conversation with him and his wife and daughter. I was treated cordially and kindly. And also as an equal. I had little to say, but I gloried in the moment.

On the last day I posed, Benton wanted to sketch my hands and asked me to take off my wristwatch. Feeling a sense of regret at the end of the experience, I was occupied with storing away every sight and sound. So when I left, I forgot the watch.

I felt I shouldn't intrude by phoning to ask if I could return and get it. Besides, it was a cheap watch and a small price to pay for being in the presence of a man I admired and respected.

A few days later, Matson told me Benton had told him to remind me I had left the watch. I was too shy to phone and ask when I could get it, yet I wouldn't go without his knowing I was coming.

A couple of weeks passed. We reached the opening night of our play. As I was in the dressing room putting on makeup, a voice behind me said, "I thought you might need this." I looked up to see a smiling Thomas Hart Benton holding my watch.

My wife has urged me a number of times to go to Lincoln University to see the mural. I never have. Standing and looking at my "likeness" could never equal the wonderful experience of posing for Thomas Hart Benton.

Published on June 23, 1996

Bicycles: a child's first one

By Sally Wilson

Children with their bicycles. Sign in spokes reads: Join Wards Bike Parade, Win a Prize.

I didn't get my first bicycle until I was 9, although I dreamed a lot about riding.

I just knew I'd be able to ride — if only I had the opportunity.

I was so envious when my girlfriend got a new Schwinn. It was 1952, and her bike was the latest thing on the market. I knew all I could do was fantasize because my family didn't have a lot of extra money.

Then one afternoon my parents left me with my older sister while they went to a police auction. I had no idea why and thought it was a bit strange.

When they returned, Dad unloaded two bicycles — one boy's and one girl's. They were sad looking, rusty with bent fenders, broken chains, torn seats and flat tires. Dad had paid $5 for both of them.

I tried to hide my disappointment.

My father and I began the tedious job of taking parts from both bicycles to make one good bike. Together we sanded and painted, replaced parts and fixed tubes. Gradually the hybrid bicycle took shape. When we finished, no one could have been prouder.

And just as I had dreamed, I got on my bike and rode like a pro.

A new world opened up for me. I rode everywhere and never thought again about my girlfriend's new Schwinn. This bike Dad and I built was so precious to me. No one could have a finer bicycle.

When the Kiwanis Club organized a bicycle rodeo at a local shopping center, I decided to enter, even though I was just a novice rider. When the events were over, I listened while the winners were announced.

"Sally Atkins — first place."

I couldn't believe my ears. I ran to the stage and claimed my trophy (which I still have to this day). I then rushed home to show my parents.

They were astonished. They had no idea I'd even entered the rodeo.

I rode that bicycle for many years, But it wasn't until much later that I realized the real treasure was not my trophy. The bicycle — and all the love that went into it — were my real prize.

I just knew I'd be able to ride —
if only I had the opportunity.

Published on June 4, 2000

Blues Stadium

By Charles Sandy

Fans watch a Kansas City Blues game in 1948 at Blues Stadium.

Blues Stadium at 22nd and Brooklyn disappeared long ago, but I recall some awfully good times there.

In the early 1950s, before the Athletics, Royals and Chiefs came to town, my friends and I from Lillis High School must have broken all records for sneaking into athletic events. We were masters at finding ways to watch for free some of the worst baseball Kansas City ever saw from 1948 to the arrival of the Royals. Sneaking into the old stadium didn't entail much thought because the Blues Stadium management simply couldn't conceive of anyone showing that much interest in the horrible teams that followed the 1947 American Association championship team.

Most illegal entry entails some sort of tool. Ours was an old railroad tie we found outside the left field stands near a section of the concrete wall that surrounded the stadium. We placed the tie at a fairly safe angle against the wall and scrambled up it, jumped down about 8 feet, scattered into the stands and met later in the empty box seats just like all the swells who never attended the games. The few ushers in the grandstand were reading *The Star* or dozing.

I suppose some readers already have classified us as delinquents for our ghastly crimes, but we preferred to think of our sneaking in as acts of charity for the fan-starved players. Also, we knew we were boosting the unofficial attendance count from 453 to maybe 459 when we were in full force.

Perhaps the one event that stands out in my memory was a late summer night in 1952 when the New York Giants and the Washington Redskins played an exhibition football game before probably 20,000 wannabe pro football fans. When we arrived at the stadium, we realized that the old railroad tie wouldn't work.

The place was crawling with guards hired to stop about 500 teen-agers from sneaking in. The guards were trying to keep bunches of boys from coming over the left-field wall on Brooklyn.

For a while they succeeded. They swung clubs at us as we stood on friends' shoulders and peeked over the wall. Being one of the lightest and not brightest, I still can feel the swish of the club under my nose.

That evening my friends and I abandoned all finesse. When the guards finally tired, we, along with hundreds of other teen-age boys, scaled the concrete barrier. We jumped to the steeply pitched hill in left field, rolled down it, then climbed back up it to a weedy spot in what amounted to end-zone seats. Not much sophistication on our part, but high standards sometimes get in the way.

We had other tools and other Kansas City targets such as Municipal Auditorium, CYC Stadium, etc. (never the water supply), but I refuse to comment any further. I fear in these nervous days that some overly serious vigilante might still consider us as threats to the national security and track me and my old friends down like Nazi war criminals, statute of limitations or not.

We preferred to think of our sneaking in as acts of charity for the fan-starved players.

Inside the old Board of Trade in 1927.

Published on November 14, 1999

Board of Trade

By Thomas G. Williams

I was hired for $65 a month to run errands.

Baltimore Avenue, looking north to the old Board of Trade Building, in 1938.

We moved from St. Louis to Kansas City in the summer of 1936, renting a large three-story house at 3705 Walnut St. The job of providing for a family of three boys, ages 14, 12 and 9, had fallen to my mother, and she was going to do the only thing she really knew how to do: keep house for us, and take in boarders to help pay the bills.

My father had lost his job with the Wabash railroad in 1934 and was put into a hospital in Illinois. Mother had been raised on the family farm in Lathrop, Mo. She wanted to be near other members of her family, so we moved to Kansas City.

We had two young people come live with us, one a pleasant young man who was going to pharmacy school, the other one of Mom's nieces, Nancy Ruth, who was going to comptometer school. The comptometer was a newfangled office machine that had just come into play in KC offices. It was similar to an adding machine but more versatile, and it required training. This kept Nancy living with us through the winter.

In spite of the boarders, things kept getting tighter and tighter, and in the spring of 1937 Mom gave up on the boarding house idea and moved us to the house on the old home place. My uncle Les Adams had purchased the farm from the estate and let us live there rent-free. We had five cows to milk for their milk and cream, which we sold for pocket money. We raised chickens for eggs and also to eat; we had wonderful fried chicken every Sunday for dinner. We raised a few pigs, butchering one every six months or so for meat to eat and lard to cook with. We chopped trees for wood for the old potbellied stove.

I graduated from Lathrop High School in the spring of 1942. The war had started, but I was only 17 and had to go to work for a few months to help Mother before I could be drafted into the Army.

I found an office boy's job with Hart, Bartlett and Sturdivant Grain Co. at 10th and Wyandotte in the old Board of Trade Building. I was hired for $65 a month to run errands. Since I needed a place to live while I worked in town, I looked in *The Star* want ads for a place to room and board. I found a widow, Mrs. Berg, who lived at 3705 Walnut — the very place my family had lived five years earlier. For $30 a month I was back in the room that my brother Ray and I had shared.

In August 1942, one month before turning 18, I volunteered for the Navy. I was sent to the Great Lakes Naval Training Station in January 1943. Life was difficult for all families during the 1930s and early 1940s, but what a glorious time, and how lucky it was for us three boys to be raised on a farm. I wouldn't have traded it for any other place in the world.

The Boulevard Drive-In in 1955.

Boulevard Drive-In

By Shirley Williams

Published on September 17, 2000

We would put a mattress in the back of our Plymouth station wagon, load up and head for the Friday-night movie.

Years ago in the late 1950s, when our children were little, one of our favorite places to go was the Boulevard Drive-In Theatre, on Southwest Boulevard in Kansas City, Kan.

For tickets, we saved soda-pop bottles until we had enough to get a couple of dollars in refunds (at 2 cents or 5 cents for each bottle). On Friday evenings, we would eat supper, bathe the kids, dress them in their jammies and make a lot of popcorn and Kool-Aid. We would put a mattress in the back of our Plymouth station wagon, load up and head for the Friday-night movie.

By the time the previews were over, the younger tots would be asleep, and we would settle down for a fun and relaxing evening.

Once in a while a nearby train noise would interrupt the movie, but no one seemed to mind.

One hot summer night, though, we were watching a Western with the usual exciting cattle drive and the cowboys rounding up the large, bellowing herd. But then we actually began smelling those cattle, and the lowing seemed more real and closer. It soon became apparent that a cattle train had derailed next to the drive-in.

The real herd roamed along the railroad tracks, a fence keeping them out of the drive-in lot. The bawling cattle let everyone know they were scared and uncomfortable, long after the first movie had ended and the second one began. By the time our evening was over, the train and the cattle were gone, but the memory of that real herd blending in with that movie will last a long time.

Published on December 11, 1994

Boxing: Dempsey v. Tunney

By Ben Nicks

Jack Dempsey, circa 1930s.

Well, do I remember when Jack Dempsey knocked out Gene Tunney in the famous and controversial 1927 "long-count" fight?

Almost.

I was a lad of 8 living with my parents in Armourdale. My uncles and a couple of their buddies from Chicago were passing through in that era's tatterdemalion version of an RV and parked in our back yard to spend a few days there. Our little four-room house barely accommodated our family of four.

They showed us an awkward gadget called a "crystal-set" radio, coils of bare copper wire wrapped around an oatmeal box. A little sliding "cat's whisker" on top could pick out frequencies from the few stations around the nation.

The big event that fall was Dempsey's attempt to regain the heavyweight title from Tunney. Armourdale was a bastion of blue-collar workers. Of course, Dempsey was their favorite, a rough, tough cowboy from Montana. Tunney was a Shakespeare-reading Easterner.

As the fight started, our little kitchen was packed with relatives and neighbors. Each man took turns listening to the single ear piece, relating the blow-by-blow account at the top of his voice to an elated audience. Even I was allowed five seconds. The noise was deafening. However, silence and a sickly pallor began to spread over the revelers. The kitchen grew somber. Dempsey clearly was getting whipped.

Then, late in the fight, "Tunney's DOWN! Tunney's DOWN!"

shouted the man at the radio. Pandemonium broke loose. The reporter shouted again and again: "Tunney's out! Tunney's out! Dempsey wins by a knockout!"

The crowd rushed outside to be met by hundreds of others pouring out from their homes, where they too had been listening. Excitement raged up and down Shawnee Avenue. "Dempsey wins! Dempsey wins!"

Of course, he didn't. Someone managed to get word in through the shouting. "The fight's still going on!" And it went on to its sad conclusion.

But for one bright and shining moment, Dempsey, the people's choice, had battered his way back to the top, at least in the hearts of his faithful supporters in Armourdale.

Of course, Dempsey was their favorite, a rough, tough cowboy from Montana. Tunney was a Shakespeare-reading Easterner.

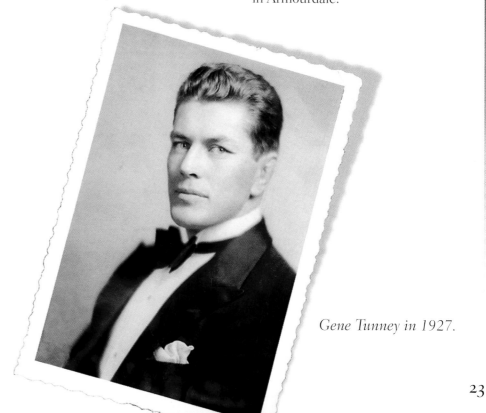

Gene Tunney in 1927.

Published on July 15, 2001

Brookside

By Mary Bauers

Bob Arfsten, left, took over the Dime Store from his father, Ernest, right. Photo from 1979.

Fanning out from the corner of 63rd Street and Brookside Boulevard are a few neighborhood shops and restaurants known to the locals simply as "Brookside." A lone picnic table and three tennis courts are to the southeast, the barbed-wire fence surrounding Border Star School's playground to the southwest, a bank to the northeast and a pharmacy to the northwest. I first rolled through this intersection in a stroller and have since crossed it innumerable times in sneakers, on bikes, on Rollerblades, in cars, on piggyback.

For me, and many of my friends and neighbors, this is not just another intersection.

Ten years ago the bank was a hardware store owned by my best friend's father. We would count our quarters and nickels and after school steal away from our mothers and our homework for Twizzlers and Blowpops at the Dime Store. During every trip we stopped at the hardware store and sat behind the cash register to flirt with the high-school cashiers.

When we started baby-sitting and earning more than our weekly allowances, we spent hours poring over the china dolls in Toy and Science, only to retreat to the Dime Store for embroidery floss every time. We sat in the one air-conditioned bedroom of my house making friendship bracelets all summer.

Later I got a job as a cashier at McDaniel's Pharmacy, where my older sisters and cousins had worked before me. I rode my bike to work that first summer; I was only 15.

When Treasury Drug bought the pharmacy in 1996, it changed. The managers changed, and the policies, and the customers. I hated working for a national corporation and quit.

After a stint as a nanny, I returned to Brookside, this time to work at Foo's Fabulous Frozen Custard, a locally owned business. Foo's operated on the familiarity that had sustained McDaniel's. We made sundaes for dogs. My friends and neighbors came in night after night. Lines snaked out the door.

With the popularity of Starbucks and Wal-Mart, I fear that establishments like Foo's and the Dime Store are a waning minority. Will my kids walk up to Brookside after school, pile onto that picnic table with their friends, pick out one piece of candy at the Dime Store and try all the science experiments at Toy and Science?

I can't promise that the Brookside shopping district will persevere through the 21st century, but I'll guarantee that there will always be a market for embroidery floss and doggy sundaes.

We would count our quarters and nickels and after school steal away from our mothers and our homework for Twizzlers and Blowpops at the Dime Store.

Published on April 6, 1997

Bucket: its many uses

By Marjorie C. Eitel

Another time I used the blue dinner bucket
to fend off a sheep that tried to butt my sister
and me as we crossed a pasture.

My grandmother bought me a light blue, metal dinner bucket when I was in first grade. In those days, most pupils carried their lunch in half-gallon pails that had been containers for sorghum molasses. So I was proud of my genuine lunch bucket and found many uses for it.

Growing up on a farm in north Missouri in the 1930s and 1940s, I walked the two miles to a one-room school. One time I was taking the shortcut home and came to a spot where I had to cross the creek on a log. One of the bigger boys stood guard on the log, refusing to allow us little kids across. Well, I hit him with my dinner bucket. His glasses broke, and he fell in the creek. I lay awake half the night worrying. Next day, I was afraid to go to school and hid in the woods. When the bell rang, I ran in quickly and took my seat. To my great relief, nothing was ever said about the incident.

Another time I used the blue dinner bucket to fend off a sheep that tried to butt my sister and me as we crossed a pasture. One good, firm hit with the bucket turned him aside, and we made a run for the gate.

That same bucket protected us again the time my little sister and I carried home a live opossum. We spotted it hanging upside down in a small hedge tree. It had pointy teeth and a vicious-looking smile. I climbed up and got it by the tail, then instructed my sister to walk close beside me and hit it with my dinner bucket if it curled up and tried to bite me; we got home without any casualties. Our dad was a hunter, and I figured he'd be proud of his girls. But when we walked in the yard with the 'possum, his reaction was surprise.

Eventually, the metal handles broke and were replaced with baling wire. I used my dinner bucket to carry home hazelnuts, hickory nuts, pretty rocks we found along the road and big blue plums from a tree we passed at a deserted house. Of course, that nifty blue dinner bucket also carried many a peanut butter sandwich, along with apples from my grandpa's trees.

Sometimes for a special treat, or maybe when supplies were low, a sandwich of homemade bread with real butter and sugar on it was tucked inside. Grandma sure knew what I needed for school, but I doubt if she ever realized how many uses I found for my trusty companion — the little blue dinner bucket.

Illustration by Lisa Morgan

Chiefs quarterback Len Dawson.

Published on September 5, 1999

Chiefs in the '60s

By Bill McCully

*Left:
Tommy Brooker
in 1969.
Right:
Lamar Hunt
in 1967.*

We might finally have a real sports team that could compete.

It's football time again. The sports pages are full of Chiefs stories. People will wear red to work on Fridays. The stadium will be packed on game day, and the interstates will be a mess two hours before and after each game. On any given block, someone will be hosting a Chiefs party. Expectations will run high. Kansas City is a football town. But it wasn't always this way.

In the early 1960s, Kansas City was a baseball town. Like most kids, my brother and I loved sports. Dad wasn't a sports fan, but luckily for us my Uncle Gene Carey is, and he would take us to the ball games. The Kansas City A's weren't much to root for, but they were all we had. We longed for a winner.

Then along came this team called the Chiefs. Texas tycoon Lamar Hunt owned the club,

and according to Uncle Gene, this guy was for real. We might finally have a real sports team that could compete. So my brother and I became Chiefs fans. We joined the "Huddle Club" and got really cool stickers for Dad's car. We also got autographed pictures of Len Dawson and Fred Arbanas in their pristine white road uniforms, and T-shirts that said we were Huddle Club members.

On Sunday afternoons Uncle Gene would pick us up and take us to the game. Parking at Sam's, we would walk into the stadium and head to the end zone where Tommy Brooker, the place kicker, would be practicing. Along with other kids there, we would try to catch his kicks in the end-zone seats, then run the ball back and hand it over the fence. Once the game started we would follow the teams up and down the sideline. The stadium was almost empty for

the first couple of seasons.

I have vivid memories of the many great players we saw: Mack Lee Hill running through the rain for a long touchdown. Jim Nance running over everyone, except Bobby Bell. Chris Burford making a fingertip catch in the end zone. Jerry Mays crushing Jack Kemp. Finally, we had a winning sports team.

Of course it's much different today. Back then the fans were mostly fathers and sons. Now it's a business and social "event," and the crowd culture has changed. Going to the games like we used to is unthinkable now. But after all these years I'm still a fan, although I watch the games on TV from home.

One other thing is also unthinkable now: It would cost Uncle Gene a whole dollar apiece to get my brother and me into the game!

Christmas, 1938

By Bill Cunningham

Petticoat Lane at Christmastime, circa 1910-1930. Looking east along 11th from Main.

For a kid growing up during the Great Depression, Christmas officially began the day after Thanksgiving, when "Monkey" Ward's catalog arrived.

Many hours were spent thumbing through the toy section, dreaming about finding your choices under the tree on Christmas morning. Money was tight, so your list had to be short: no more than three toys, with the hope that you'd get one.

In 1938, when I was 9, my top three choices were Silver Streak ice skates; a boy's Hawthorne bike with New Departure brakes, so I wouldn't have to ride my sister Sally's bike (it had a skirt guard!); and a Stream Line steam-type electrical train with remote control that allowed you, the engineer, to speed the train forward, whistle blowing and red lights flashing, or reverse the switch so the train could back up slowly to couple cars.

Common sense told me the bike was way out of Santa's budget. The train was also pretty pricey. The skates were cheapest, so that's what I figured I'd get.

Laboriously and very neatly, I wrote my letter to Santa. I took the letter to school and, miracle of miracles, was selected to broadcast to the North Pole by way of radio station KXYZ, high atop the Kansas City Power & Light Building. Daddy took me to the station, and I sat up real close to the mike so Santa could hear me loud and clear all the way up at the North Pole. I also hoped that my mother, sisters and the whole Northeast neighborhood would know what I wanted most that year.

The magical countdown to Christmas continued. Mother took Sally and me downtown on the streetcar to marvel at all the goodies in the department store windows and to get in line to see Santa.

Christmas cards were arriving daily (they took 3-cent stamps, and mail was delivered twice a day). Mother would put them in a special basket for the family to read.

We'd go sledding down Windsor Hill, then warm up with cocoa at home. There was some snooping in closets for mysterious packages.

At Gladstone School, decorations were made and tacked up. Special Christmas programs were rehearsed. Finding the right gift for the teacher was a top priority.

At last it was Christmas Eve! Our long brown stockings were hung on the mantel of the fireplace in the front bedroom. We tried to sleep, keeping one eye open to see if Santa managed to make it down the very small chimney.

Christmas came on Sunday that year. We were up at 6:30 to peer through the banisters at the most wondrous sight downstairs: gaily wrapped packages all around the tree.

And there, ready to plug in, was my electric train. I'd learn years later that my mother bought the train in the Bargain Room of Montgomery Ward's on Christmas Eve, when toys were 50 percent off.

It was my most unforgettable Christmas, and 62 years later I'm still enjoying that train.

Mother took Sally and me downtown on the streetcar to marvel at all the goodies in the department store windows and to get in line to see Santa.

Published on November 26, 2000

Christmas, 1950s

By Jean Opfer

Christmas parade in downtown Kansas City.

When I was growing up on a farm south of Higginsville, Mo., I was blessed to live near a household of several maiden aunts and my grandmother. My brother and I, being the youngest of the nieces and nephews on that side of the family, were pampered by them, to say the least.

Around Thanksgiving we would begin mentioning things we wanted for Christmas, knowing there was a good chance of being spoiled some more. One year I asked for a bride doll, and my favorite doll, Audrey (named after Audrey Meadows of "The Jackie Gleason Show"), disappeared for two weeks or so before Christmas. On Christmas morning, Audrey was under the tree attired in an elegant bridal gown (made from an aunt's satin slip), long veil and new white shoes, carrying a miniature white Bible, bridal bouquet and tiny white lace handkerchief.

Sometime in December, usually on a school day, I was allowed to accompany an aunt or two on an annual Christmas shopping trip to downtown Kansas City. We would travel by Greyhound bus west on old Highway 40, arriving in Kansas City so early that the great department stores had not yet opened. So we would visit the bus station's coffee shop and enjoy cinnamon rolls and hot tea served in little china pots.

Then we would trek briskly downtown to begin our glorious day of shopping, taking plenty of time to enjoy the animated figures, winter and holiday scenes and lavish displays of gift items in store windows. The noise of policemen's whistles, vehicles' air brakes, and bus and delivery truck engines, and the aromas of coffee shops, traffic exhaust fumes and my aunts' favorite colognes are still vivid. December wind and the drafts created by the tall buildings kept us moving quickly from store to store.

One year I had my picture taken on Santa's lap at Emery, Bird, Thayer. I was the round-faced farm girl wearing the home-sewn slacks under my skirt (jeans were never worn on these special trips to the city). Santa's white beard and red outfit were so beautiful, and he was so kind.

Lunch was eaten at the Hawthorn Room of the Jones Store or at the Forum cafeteria. These places offered more choices than I even knew existed; selecting more than we could eat was part of the routine. After lunch we would shop some more, saving the dime stores for last, where small gifts were purchased for the aunts and grandmother left at home.

In the late afternoon we would lug our shopping bags back to the bus station for the trip home. That ride always seemed shorter than the morning one, for I would sleep most of the way.

Talking to Santa.

We would trek briskly downtown to begin our glorious day of shopping.

Enjoying the downtown Christmas windows in 1971.

Published on December 17, 2000

Christmas, 1975

By Maryann Gardner

Michael was mesmerized by the beautiful gold crowns that hung in the center of each intersection and swayed back and forth in the chilly breeze.

Gold crowns decorate downtown intersections in 1971.

On Dec. 24, 1975, my husband and I and our son were planning to drive to Iowa to spend Christmas with my mother. Four-year-old Michael was apprehensive about Santa finding him that night.

Since it would be a short work day, Michael and I rode in with my husband to his job in downtown Kansas City. We would leave for Iowa from there.

After breakfast at the Dixon Inn coffee shop, Michael and I wandered the streets and stores enjoying Christmas in Kansas City. Michael was mesmerized by the beautiful gold crowns that hung in the center of each inter-section and swayed back and forth in the chilly breeze. To his delight, as the Salvation Army band played "Joy to the World" in front of Macy's, one of the women handed him her tambourine to shake.

Since he was one of few children downtown that day, he won attention from every street-corner Santa we passed. Michael talked to each. Surprisingly, he didn't mention his concern about being

away on Christmas Eve.

Soon we were riding the Jones Store Christmas train through the "Winter Wonderland." When the ride ended, Michael climbed into the lap of the resident Santa, a man who became well-known during those years due to his jolly, convincing manner with children.

Santa being an attentive listener, he welcomed us with, "Hi, Michael. I thought you might stop by today!" At Santa's invitation, Michael told his Christmas wishes.

Then he looked up into Santa's eyes and whispered, "But Santa, I'm afraid you won't find me this Christmas."

Santa stopped short. "Why?"

"I won't be home. I'll be at Grandma's."

In a grand gesture, Santa reached behind his chair and pulled out a book almost the size of Michael. As he began to write, he said, "Michael will be at Grandma's — now, which Grandma is that again?"

"Grandma Haas," Michael said, "in Iowa."

"Ah, yes," Santa smiled. "Grandma Haas in Iowa. I know where she lives. She's a friend of mine."

His face beaming, Michael hugged Santa and jumped off his lap.

It was time for lunch, so we headed for Macy's Tea Room. The crowd was sparse, but the presence of a child seemed to add to the holiday mood for the staff. Everyone asked Michael what he wanted for Christmas, or if he'd been a good boy. Michael happily answered all queries. When it was time for ice cream, the chef himself proudly served it, proclaiming it was "for the little boy who made this a pleasant lunch."

When my husband joined us, Michael told him, "We met lots of Santa's helpers. But only the real Santa knew my Grandma Haas."

Twenty-five years later, Michael says he vaguely recalls the holiday crowns and the train ride. However, he vividly remembers the real Santa, who knew a 4-year-old's first name and was a friend of his Grandma Haas.

After the Convention Hall fire, 1900.

Published on April 2, 2000

Convention Hall: the fire

By Walter "Barney" McCray

It was April 4, 1900, a pleasant spring day that was to be memorable in the history of a thriving, energetic city. My parents had been married less than two months. Father worked at the stockyards, and Mother worked half days as a stock girl at Bernheimer's Store at the northeast corner of 12th and Main streets. They lived at 1425 Washington.

Her day's work completed, Mother was walking home for her lunch and housekeeping chores. As she turned south at the corner of 12th and Central, she walked on the covered sidewalk that was part of Convention Hall, a grand new building that was less than a year old and had been chosen by the Democratic Party as the site of its national convention.

Before she reached 13th Street, children playing in the yard of Lathrop School on the west side of Central yelled across to her: "Lady, you better get out from there; that building is on fire." At first she thought it was just a child's joke, but in minutes she realized the truth when Chief Hale's world-famous fire laddies arrived from their station just two blocks away.

Mother went across the street to the southwest corner of 13th and Central from where she watched the magnificent building disappear in flames. The story of how it was rebuilt in 90 days to house the Democrats is well-known Kansas City history. If it happened today, our City Council would probably still be "in committee."

Convention Hall held many wonderful memories for me in later years. I recall Teddy Roosevelt's visit in 1918, when he addressed an overflow crowd in the Hall. While our mothers sat in the back row of the balcony, Bud Tytler and I climbed up to get a better view on the steel girders that supported the ceiling. Teddy's booming voice held the audience spellbound.

One year, at Christmastime, a silent version of "Snow White" was shown on a gigantic four-sided screen suspended from the ceiling high above the arena floor.

The high school basketball games every year were sellouts. Kansas City had four high schools so there were two games each Friday night. Two round robins were played so that meant eight exciting nights of basketball. After the game we bought doughnuts on 12th Street to eat on the streetcar as we rode home.

In the early 1920s, Kansas City was the mecca for championship wrestling, which was far different from today's farce. With such names as Joe Stecher, famous for his "scissor hold," Ed "Strangler" Lewis, Frank Gotch, Jim Londos and Stanislaus Zybysko. I didn't go, but Father said the air was so full of cigar smoke you could cut it with a knife.

To a kid beginning a lifelong fascination with motor cars, the annual auto show was excitement to look forward to.

Yes, the old hall fills many chapters in my growing-up memories of Kansas City.

Published on August 20, 2000

Cowboy heroes: Gene Autry

By Don Farley

The passing away of so many cowboy film heroes in the last two years brings to mind summers in Kansas City, Kan., in the late 1940s and 1950s. All of us youngsters in my neighborhood would head to the Jayhawk Theatre at 18th and Central Avenue. Each Saturday we could watch two great B Western movies, 10 cartoons and a serial.

The kids would start ganging up in front of the box office about noon. The admission for the entire program was 15 cents, and you could get a Coke for 5 cents and a box of popcorn for 5 cents.

When my parents could afford it, they would give my brother and me 50 cents each, which meant extra popcorn, Cokes and candy bars. The owners of the theater always had a gimmick of some kind, where they would read a telegram from Roy Rogers or Gene Autry to all the excited kids. The kids all thought the "Howdy, pardners" message was directed right to them. Many of us would stay over and watch the second show. The old Jayhawk Theatre is gone now, replaced in the 1960s by the Chas. Balls market, which still stands.

Those Saturday movies certainly kept us kids out of trouble. Those cowboy heroes of yesteryear were a parent's dream — the good guys didn't drink, smoke or cuss! Those great old Western movies were morality plays; today's movies, on the other hand, seem to be immorality plays.

Yes, the cowboy heroes are almost all gone now, but memories of those summer Saturdays at the Jayhawk remain.

Those cowboy heroes of yesteryear were a parent's dream — the good guys didn't drink, smoke or cuss!

...wboy Gene Autry.

Published on February 11, 1996

Delivery wagon, 1920s

By Dorothy Bogart

Delivery wagon in Independence in the 1920s.

How well I remember the little horse-drawn wagon that delivered ice blocks every few days throughout my childhood to our home in Independence.

You see, we did not own a refrigerator back in the 1920s. Like most folks, our perishable foods were kept, literally, in an icebox out on the back porch.

The outside of the box was wood. Ours resembled a small trunk. An ice block was placed in the bottom to keep the food chilled.

Naturally, the ice gradually melted. That's why the ice man and his regular deliveries were such an important part of neighborhood life.

On each appointed day, my mother would place a white cardboard square in our dining room window, where the delivery man could see it easily from the street.

The card was printed with four large numbers, one on each edge: 25, 50, 75, 100. The number my mother put at the top indicated the pounds of ice we needed that day.

The delivery man routinely hauled 100-pound ice blocks in his wagon. These blocks were scored, so he could separate them easily into smaller pieces if necessary. He clamped large tongs onto the ice chunk and lugged it to our box on the back porch.

In summer, neighborhood children especially looked forward to the ice wagon's visits. The kindly driver usually kept a special block from which he chipped pieces to give to his young followers.

These ice chips were real treats on hot summer days.

My how times have changed. Gleaming refrigerators turned the icebox and delivery man into nothing more than childhood memories.

But at least back then we didn't have to worry about a power failure.

Our neighborhood ice-delivery wagon was faithful, no matter the season. And our sturdy icebox kept food from spoiling — without any assistance from electricity.

You see, we did not own a refrigerator back in the 1920s.

Joltin' Joe DiMaggio of the New York Yankees.

Published on January 10, 1999

DiMaggio

By Angelo Bongino

*Everything I had
planned to say to
DiMaggio slipped
my mind.*

As a teen-ager, I yearned to meet my favorite sports figure face to face. The opportunity came in the summer of 1949.

That year my cousin Jay and I were outfielders for a Don Bosco Center 3&2 baseball team — and devout New York Yankee fans. We lit up like bottle rockets when we heard they were coming to town to play their farm team, the Kansas City Blues. That meant a chance to meet my hero, Joe DiMaggio.

I kept a scrapbook covering his postwar career, but DiMaggio articles were scarce the first half of 1949. He had spent that period recovering from surgery on a bone spur beneath one heel and had missed all of spring training and half the regular season.

In late June, Yanks manager Casey Stengel decided to test Joe's heel in a crucial three-game series with the Red Sox in Fenway Park. Joe responded with four homers. The Yankees swept the series; fans and sportswriters buzzed about the comeback.

Days before the Kansas City game, I dreaded that I might not see Joe play because the Yanks might not start him for fear of reinjuring him in a no-brainer exhibition. So Jay and I decided on a way to circulate among the Yankees off the field.

The morning of the game, we floated about the main lobby of the Muehlebach Hotel amid a swarm of Yanks checking in. We hustled a number of autographs, mostly from ex-Blues: Phil Rizzuto, Al Rosen, Jerry Coleman, Cliff Mapes. We didn't see Joe D. among them.

Just as we were about to give up, I spotted him atop the mezzanine steps, seated in the shade of a tall potted plant. Next to him was Joe Page, Yankees relief pitcher.

Jay and I rushed up to them and suddenly froze. Everything I had planned to say to DiMaggio slipped my mind. Finally I mentioned the scrapbook. Joe smiled at me and said something, I can't recall what. I handed him a copy of "Lucky to Be a Yankee," his autobiography. He signed it, as did Page.

With our autographs secure, Jay and I stood gaping at the broad-shouldered Joe in his two-piece suit. Quietly we backed away as you would in the presence of royalty.

Jay and I took in the game at Blues Stadium. When DiMaggio was on the field, I studied his every graceful move. He left the lineup after a couple of innings. After that the game went flat for me. I never saw DiMaggio in person again.

I lost the scrapbook, but I still have the autograph, which was a good-luck token for me: My Yanks won a Pennant and World Series that year, and our 3&2 club grabbed the Midget "A" North Division title.

Dixon Hotel in 1923, at 12th and Baltimore.

Published on May 2, 1999

Dixon Hotel

By Loree Achenbach

Each summer beginning in the 1940s, my parents loaded me and my brother and sister into the family sedan for our annual trip to Kansas City for a weekend of shopping, going to a movie and eating out. We always stayed in the Dixon Hotel on 12th Street in the heart of downtown.

The first time I saw the Dixon, I couldn't believe that we were going to stay in such a building. I'd never seen anything like it except in the movies. The marble lobby was the biggest room I had ever been in, and it was always filled with a crowd of people milling about, more people than I could imagine in one place. I can still remember gripping my mother's hand with all my strength.

We were from Hoisington, Kan., a town of about 3,000 in the central part of the state. The main sources of income for Hoisington were the railroad, oil wells, farming and cattle. Although many of the cattlemen made frequent visits to the stockyards in Kansas City to buy and/or sell, we were "town people" and didn't have those business reasons for trips to the city. But it was important to my parents that we grow beyond the bounds of the small town where we lived, and going to KC was part of that vision.

Each visit we ate at least one of our meals at the Forum Cafeteria on Main Street. The first time we were there, the sight of rows of food stretching before us must have caused my mind to shut down. I eventually found myself at the end of the line with a tray of food so heavy I couldn't carry it. My brother and sister had a similar experience.

After that first trip Mother made the rule that each of us had to eat everything on our trays. The next time, my little brother took one small bowl of carrots — he didn't even like them — and nothing else.

The highlight of these trips for my mother was the mandatory visit to the Cinderella shop, a shoe store that had a large selection of the size $4^1/_2$ shoes she wore. Without Cinderella she would have had to mail-order unfashionable styles from the catalogs. It's been 40 years since the last visit to Cinderella, and Mother still has the pair of jeweled sandals she purchased on that trip.

The clearest recollection of those trips for my brother and sister is the vision of those lines of food in the Forum; to this day, they both believe they haven't been in a comparable cafeteria. The highlight for my father was getting everyone home without losing anyone or having car problems. And what I remember most is the grand lobby of the Dixon.

Published on December 21, 1997

Downtown elegance

By Mary Hecht

About 500 people attended the premiere of the Terrace Grill at the Muehlebach Hotel in 1936.

The words that come to mind when I recall the downtown area in the 1940s are: elegant, romantic, memorable.

I was a young secretary working in the Bryant Building at 11th and Grand, which was on what was known as Petticoat Lane. There was a wide variety of eating and shopping places to enjoy at lunch hour. Within two blocks there were wonderful stores — Harzfeld's, John Taylor, Peck's and Kline's, to name a few. And who could forget the Jones Store with its Hawthorne Room, where the gracious waitresses wore their smart uniforms and aprons. My mother and I enjoyed it so much, and later I would take my children to eat there. They still experience nostalgia when we mention it.

Then there was Emery, Bird, Thayer with its tearoom on the balcony and its mezzanine with comfortable chairs where one could rest while shopping. You could purchase yarn there, and a nice lady taught you to knit.

Christmastime downtown was especially magical, people hurrying through the cold from store to store, enjoying the sounds of carols and the Salvation Army bell ringers. Perhaps because I was young I remember people smiling more then.

Entertainment spots and restaurants were abundant — the Terrace Grill at the Muehlebach, the Drum Room at the Hotel President, Downtowner Lounge, Pink Elephant and, of course, the Italian Gardens, where the style and quality are still the same.

Our country was at war, and patriotism was strong. On any given day, a platform would be set up on the street, where a military band and a singer would inspire the sale of war bonds. When the first B-25 bombers were built at the Fairfax Plant, they created a lot of excitement when one took off over the city. Being a part of the crowd on 12th Street the night the war ended was unforgettable.

I wish my children's children could enjoy downtown as we did.

Entertainment spots and restaurants were abundant — the Terrace Grill at the Muehlebach, the Drum Room at the Hotel President, Downtowner Lounge, Pink Elephant and, of course, the Italian Gardens, where the style and quality are still the same.

Published on October 12, 1997

Downtown shopping

By Patsy White

Twelfth Street in the early 1940s.

I was 10 years old in 1939. We lived in St. Joseph. My dad worked anywhere he could to take care of his family, including for the Works Progress Administration. My mother worked at the Douglas Candy Factory. I remember her coming home smelling like chocolate. Sometimes she would have a few pieces in her pocket for us. It was quite a treat. On Saturday my mother would iron clothes, and my dad would turn on the radio to listen to the Vine Street Varieties from Kansas City. This is my first memory of Kansas City and of wishing I could go there.

In 1941 my dad was working at the Sunflower Ordnance Plant in Eudora, Kan. I'll never forget the day he told us we were moving to Kansas City. I was so happy. I thought we would be living Downtown where all the lights were, but instead Dad said it was a trailer camp with cabins that were partly furnished. We started packing what we could into our 1936 Ford and headed down Highway 169.

Eventually we could see the outline of the town and all the lights. That was my first view of Kansas City. When we got to the camp, our cabin was one big room with two beds, a small table and chairs, and a hot plate to cook on. Mother later made a cabinet out of an orange crate for dishes. We lived in the camp for seven years. During that time there was a man that would show Western movies out in the yard. We had some good times, especially when my mother, sister and I would go shopping Downtown. I had been working at National Bellas Hess making 40 cents an hour, so I had money to spend. There were Grant's, Peck's, Kline's, Macy's, Jones and Woolworth and Kresge, where I would get a chili dog and a root beer for lunch. My brother also worked at National Bellas Hess; he had to wear roller skates because the building was so long.

When I graduated my parents bought me a corsage at Ed's Florist at 31st and Gillham. And I used to ride the streetcar to El Torreon Skating and the Pla-Mor. They also had a walkathon that lasted several weeks. We would go up on Cliff Drive and drink the spring water. We would go to Fairyland Park, where at the penny arcade you could get your picture taken for 24 cents. There was a man that sold hot tamales from a cart by Sears at 15th and Cleveland, where I also worked.

Now they are restoring everything at 18th and Vine. It's like history repeating all over again.

We had some good times, especially when my mother, sister and I would go shopping Downtown.

The Kresge dime store lunch counter, in 1951.

Published on January 30, 2000

Downtown Thursdays

By Marilyn Harville

Harzfeld's department store at 11th and Main, in 1951.

Five weeks into my junior year of high school, in September 1944, I moved to Kansas City with my mother and a sister. Our new home was an apartment on Armour Boulevard, where an older sister already lived. The architecture of the beautiful apartment buildings along the boulevard was a sight to behold to a 16-year-old from a very small town.

I enrolled at Westport High School. Having come from a class of approximately 30 to a class of more than 300 was a rather frightening but awesome experience. Things do have a way of working out, however, and Westport turned out to be a good place to finish my high school education.

When weather permitted, I walked to school. I would walk down Armour Boulevard to Gillham and then through Gillham Park to school. This walk to and from school was a favorite part of the day for me. The park was beautiful, and I enjoyed it in all seasons. I even liked walking in the rain (when it was raining lightly) and listening to the rain coming down through the trees. It was my time for communing with nature and daydreaming — as most 16-year-olds are wont to do.

Since I was the first of our family to get home in the afternoon, I would walk to the little Italian market two blocks away to get our groceries for the evening meal. We had an account there, so all I had to do was hand them my list, and they did the rest. By shopping every day, there was never too much for me to carry.

Thursday nights were special. That is when all the stores stayed open until 9. My mother worked at Emery, Bird, Thayer and one sister worked at Harzfeld's, so on Thursdays I would meet my older sister, who worked for an insurance company. I would take the Armour-Paseo bus to 11th and Baltimore and meet her in front of her building.

We would do some shopping and eat dinner downtown. There was lots of variety in eating places downtown in those days: the Hawthorne Room at the Jones Store; the Myron Green Cafeteria; the Forum; Emery, Bird, Thayer's tearoom; and the lunch counters at the Katz and Parkview drugstores and the Woolworth and Kresge dime stores.

Kansas City was where I would meet my future husband (now deceased), a dental student at the University of Kansas City School of Dentistry, then at 10th and Troost. But that's another story.

Published on April 23, 2000

Easter chicks

By Virginia Sandy McLaury

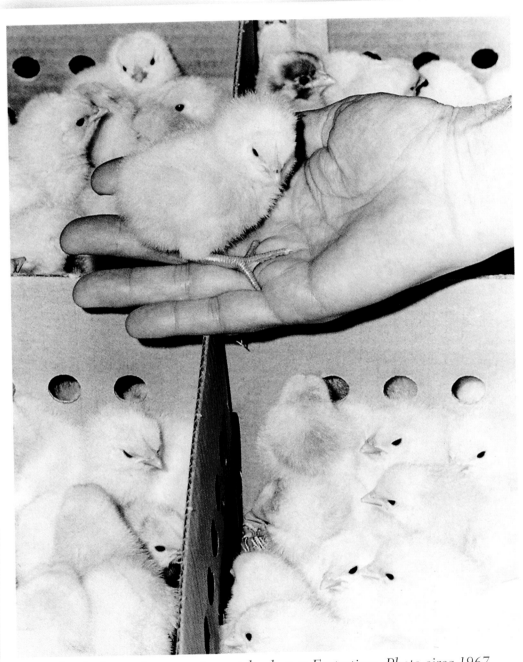

Baby chicks used to come in pastel colors at Eastertime. Photo circa 1967.

For many years my mother and father would go to Katz Drug store and buy us a pet for Easter. You could buy baby chicks whose down feathers had been dyed pastel colors and undyed yellow ducks. Now this was the "olden days," so I hope the Society for the Prevention of Cruelty to Animals doesn't call me.

We first got two chicks we named Fibber McGee and Molly. When they were little, we carried them all over the house wrapped in old towels for hygienic reasons. Besides, my mother would really holler if we didn't. But sometimes we let them loose in the house and at one point, they were lost. We could hear them peeping but couldn't find them. My grandpa, who lived with us, was walking all around asking where the *$\&$ chicks were. Fortunately, they were rescued from the bottom of a cold air shaft where they had fallen. The chicks died young, probably because they were dyed. We buried them in the back yard, each with a rock tombstone.

We switched to pet ducks after that. They were always named Quack or Quack Quack. When they got big, they resided in the back yard, sharing it with our dog Butch. In the fall we took them to the ponds at Loose Park or Penn Valley Park and released them. We would go back later to visit, always thinking we recognized "our" duck from the others. Some met accidental deaths and were buried along with the chicks. They all made really good pets, following us all over the neighborhood. One even followed my sister to the bus stop when she was going to high school. The ducks never bothered anybody, and the neighbors didn't seem to mind them.

That is, they didn't mind them except for one duck.

I think he came from a bad seed. He pestered and stole food scraps from the dog, who had really put up with all the others because of his good heart. And that Quack despised me. My brother admits now that he taught the duck to attack me. Every time I set foot in the back yard, the duck came after me, chasing me and pecking my bare legs. I distinctly remember standing on the top of a metal garbage can yelling for someone to call off the duck.

Well, one Sunday when we were walking home from church, it happened. As we approached the house, we saw duck feathers all over. When we got to the back yard, Butch the dog was sunning himself on the driveway, and I saw him wink at me. No remains were ever found. But Butch and I know what happened. In the end, that Quack got his.

*My grandpa, who lived with us, was walking all around asking where the *$\&$ chicks were.*

The Manor Bread wagon, making deliveries in 1941.

Published on September 26, 1999

East Side

By Peggy Todd Short

Vegetable and fruit hucksters, the Manor Bread horse-drawn wagon and the hot-tamale cart came by regularly.

When I was growing up in the 1930s, the East Side of Kansas City was my world. I lived between the 24th Street streetcar line and 27th Street. Early one hot August morning in 1930, Mama said it was my birthday. I was 4 years old. I hurried outside to tell the neighbor kids, who later "surprised" Mama by showing up in our back yard to play and help turn the handle on the ice-cream freezer. That same year in October, my baby sister was born.

Walking was our chief means of transportation on the East Side. We walked to church, Phoenix Park Methodist at 26th and Spruce, and to school, Ashland grade school, 24th and Elmwood, and East High School. Usually we walked home from Ashland for lunch.

One snowy day when I was in first grade Daddy brought my galoshes to me at school. "I didn't know your father was a motorman," my teacher said. "Motorman" was a new word for me so I replied: "No, he's a streetcar man!"

One summer day while still a grade-schooler I walked to the library at East High to check out books. It was a long mile from home, but reading was fun for me. The librarian remarked that I was "ambitious."

Mama usually bought groceries at Sugarwater's at 27th and Jackson. They delivered and also gave credit. We kept a card in the front window so the ice man knew when we needed ice. Vegetable and fruit hucksters, the Manor Bread horse-drawn wagon and the hot-tamale cart came by regularly.

The strect always shook when fire trucks roared by from 24th and Spruce.

A summer treat was when men turned on fire hydrants at the corners. In winter the two steep hills on 25th Street were great for sledding. Someone always had to keep watch for cars. We could roller skate on the sidewalks and, when we got older, play ball in the streets.

My sister and I loved going to the movies at the Ashland theater most Friday nights and sometimes on Sunday afternoons. Kids paid a dime; adults paid 20 cents. Sometimes Mama took us to catch the streetcar to go downtown. At Kresge dime store I enjoyed listening to the lady play sheet music on the piano. A new hair ribbon and a chocolate soda made my day. After many years and many changes I still enjoy remembering the way it was on the old East Side.

Published on February 12, 1995

Fairyland Park

By John Gratton

Fairyland Park in the 1940s.

In the late 1950s, Fairyland Park was *the* amusement park in Kansas City. It was, as the bold said, a magical sort of place for the bold. And it wasn't such a bad place for cowards either — if you found the arcade games before you found the roller coaster.

That coaster was long and tall and made of wood. It seemed about as stable as a 12-story house of cards in a tornado. But it wasn't the roller coaster that caused my blood to run cold; it simply terrorized me.

No, what caused my blood to run cold — to freeze into slush — was the Dutch Shoes, a ride for those who might rush in where angels fear to tread. The two containers (shoes) were lifted, then dropped in an arc that grew until they were suspended upside down in midair.

From that precarious position, the shoes were tilted over ever so slowly and then rushed earthward, only to go all the way to the top again and again, until you had to be on the verge of dying or hoping you were on the verge of dying. I spent much of my youth avoiding Fairyland's Dutch Shoes, like a saint avoids sin. Until 1959, that is.

That summer my friend, Jimmy, a kid destined to become a jet pilot, talked me into a trip on the Dutch Shoes. He did it the way things could sometimes be done in the '50s. He called me a chicken. He then pointed to two kids half our 16 years boarding one shoe, leaving the other open.

Before I had a chance to say a perfect act of contrition, I was suspended in midair listening to a horrendous screech, a gut-wrenching yell that I mistook for my own cry of terror. Instead the shrieks of anguish were coming from the two kids in the other death trap. It was a horrid wail that I could have matched if I hadn't been too petrified to scream.

At last the operator had had enough of their fearful cries and brought us down. "I'm sorry," he said to Jimmy and me, "I had to stop the ride."

While I offered prayers of thanksgiving, Jimmy protested that he and I shouldn't be penalized for what a couple of 8-year-olds lacked.

"You're right," the operator said. "You can go again."

And he started our free ride, which seemed to last forever.

I was suspended in midair listening to a horrendous screech, a gut-wrenching yell that I mistook for my own cry of terror.

Lined up to eat at the Forum Cafeteria, in the 1940s.

Published on May 18, 1997

Forum Cafeteria

By Sue Meyer Wright

By the time I reached the cashier, my tray was loaded with mashed potatoes and brown gravy, hamsteak with cherry sauce, a biscuit and butter and chocolate milk.

Like a lot of Kansas City families, mine celebrated birthdays downtown at the Forum Cafeteria. From the moment one of us opted for dinner and a show rather than pin-the-tail-on-the-donkey, we began anticipating the car ride to the city, choosing the perfect picture show, and pushing into the Forum in our Cinderella dresses.

Dining at the Forum was no small task for a young child. Good manners were challenged the minute we arrived and salvaged only by our parents' watchful supervision.

With the maze of dream food just steps away, my sister and I fell into position between our parents. Dad already had said we could choose anything we wanted but we would be expected to eat everything on our plate. As we reached for a tray and the heavy silverware stowed in starchy linen, he smiled as if to say: "Don't let your eyes get bigger than your stomach."

Being the oldest child, I moved to first in line and bore the responsibility for our momentum down the course. Perhaps it was my sensitive nature, but the serving ladies always looked stern. Sometimes the meat lady screamed out "Next!" before I had time to negotiate with the vegetable person.

I always started with the same items — cubes of red Jell-O for salad and cubes of green Jell-O for dessert. In truth, I never liked lime Jell-O, but I could not resist its color and the knowledge that this was my only opportunity to have Jell-O in cubes of any color.

When I arrived at the real desserts, I was crushed: I loved the syrupy strawberry shortcake with whipped cream, but only the most pitiful birthday pout and a pledge to eat every bite could finagle that last addition.

By the time I reached the cashier, my tray was loaded with mashed potatoes and brown gravy, hamsteak with cherry sauce, a biscuit and butter and chocolate milk. She would figure my total, place the tab on the tray, then ask the critical question, "Will you need help, young lady?"

Carrying your own tray was a rite of passage to a young girl. My parents let me decide when I was ready to be a "big girl," and although I ran the gantlet without mishap, I still remember the wiggly weight of the tray and my relief in setting it down.

My sister and I could be counted on to cry halfway through the meal that we were getting full. That was our parents' cue to respond with, "You know what we said!" After we forced a few more bites, they would relent and Dad would dutifully finish whatever was left, including the green Jell-O.

I would love to relive one of those birthdays of my youth, again leading my mother, father and sister at the proper pace, through the cubes of Jell-O and the mashed potatoes and gravy and the strawberry shortcake.

But it would still probably require a pitiful pout and the loving indulgence of two very sweet parents.

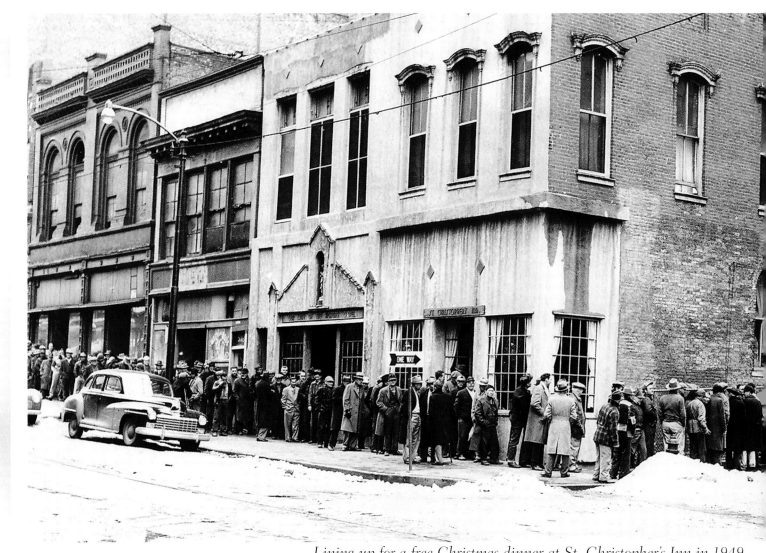

Lining up for a free Christmas dinner at St. Christopher's Inn in 1949.

Hard times

By Kathleen Murphy

There were many men who came to our house asking for work to do for something to eat.

My oldest brother, Chester, was born June 26, 1908, which meant he came of age during the 1929 Depression. After a fruitless job search in Kansas City, he joined the evergrowing ranks of young and old who were riding the rails in search of job opportunities.

He would be gone for months, then suddenly show up with sanitized tales of life on the road, hobo jungles and the dangerous crossing of Death Valley.

Early one Christmas morning, I came downstairs to see what Santa had brought, and there sat Chester at the kitchen table having a cup of coffee with our father. Chester would sit beside me and tell me how much I had grown since he had last seen me and how much prettier I had gotten.

I loved to listen to him tell about the places he had been and the sights he had seen. I knew that when I grew up I wanted to see the snow-capped top of Pikes Peak. I wanted to see the ocean and watch the waves come in and pick up seashells.

There were many men who came to our house asking for work to do for something to eat. It was usually older men. I guess the younger ones found other ways of getting food. My father had built a bench and set it just outside the kitchen door. When a man came asking for food, my mother would ask him to sit on the bench, and she would fix a large bologna sandwich or a peanut-butter-and-jelly sandwich and a tall glass of milk. If I were home, she would ask me to take it out to the gentleman.

I learned that hobos marked houses where they could always get something to eat. One day my friend Marjorie asked, "Why does your mother give food to every hobo who comes to your door?"

"Doesn't your mother?" I asked.

"Sometimes we just don't answer the door and we pretend no one is home," she replied.

One day I asked my mother why she didn't ever turn down anyone when they asked for food.

Her voice was steady, but her eyes filled with tears.

"I hope there is a mother out there who will always give my son a bite to eat," she said.

Published on May 25, 1997

Hats

By Ruth Weislocher

Hat styles from 1956, 1961, 1963.

1956

1963

1961

1956

1956

"Do you remember when we sat around a bridge table wearing hats?"

The question brought a roar of laughter and a flood of conversation that temporarily halted the friendly afternoon bridge game at both tables. All the women there remembered when they wore hats for nearly all important occasions: luncheons and meetings, parties and funerals, visiting and traveling.

No dress-up outfit was complete without a hat. Every style-conscious female wanted a new hat for spring, especially for church. (Sometimes the inspection of the parade of stylish headgear was more engrossing than the song, sermon or prayer.)

Fifty years ago, shopping for a new spring outfit meant visiting the millinery department of your favorite ladieswear shop, where a variety of attractive chapeaux were displayed on individual stands like blossoms on a stem. Spring hats were made of straw; white, black or brightly colored, and usually trimmed with silky flowers, ribbon bows or streamers, or even a small veil.

Ladies sat in front of a mirror while a clerk assisted them in adjusting a hat to just the proper angle. Choosing a style that was compatible with your hairstyle and several spring costumes was tricky and time-consuming. Some stores had a milliner who would shape and trim a hat especially for you. For a few extra dollars, you could have an original creation. An old hat could be made to look new by adding new ribbons, flowers or a mesh veil.

Hat styles varied from season to season. The pillbox worn on the back of the head was made famous by Jackie Kennedy. A wide-brimmed straw sailor hat worn forward on the head shadowed the face and tended to minimize signs of aging. The beret worn slightly to the side of the head complemented tailored clothing, and a replica of the derby worn by equestrians was favored by more daring women. A "half hat" was just that, held to the head by a wire clip covered with flowers, feathers or ribbons. Most styles required a hat pin to hold the hat at the correct angle and to keep it from blowing away in a strong wind. Little girls wore bonnets or sailors hats trimmed with ribbon streamers.

In this era of casual, unisex and bizarre dressing, it might be fun to get dressed up from head to toe for a special occasion, but I'm sure once would be enough. For today's females, young and not so young, an attractive hairstyle is their crowning glory. Hats, once so popular and indispensable, don't fit the lifestyle of today's active women, except for the visor worn on the tennis court or golf course.

That's just fine, though, because reminiscing about the times when we loved our fancy hats is more fun than wearing them!

Choosing a style that was compatible with your hairstyle and several spring costumes was tricky and time-consuming.

Horace Mann Elementary, circa 1930s.

Published on July 16, 2000

Horace Mann neighborhood

By Bob Line

In the summer of 1937, the dust was thick on our front yard at 3711 Wabash. The water sprinkling from the hose just disappeared, and the dust floated on top. It was hot and had been hot for weeks.

Our neighborhood had plenty for a young boy to do in the summer, though, and plenty of opportunities to earn a little spending money.

Saturday mornings, we would walk with our friend Isadore Goldberg to his synagogue at 39th and Montagall. Once his rabbi even let us watch him "kosher" chickens. That was when we guys learned that we had all been "koshered" as babies. Then it was on to the Oak Park Theater on Prospect to sack candy for the kiddies' matinee, and for that we got to stay for the movie and the serials. Remember actor Noah Berry Jr.?

Sunday afternoons, we would be over at Burris Jenkins' church at Linwood and Forest for a movie. The balcony was the favorite place, and we would put a nickel,

perhaps a dime, in the collection plate. The First Baptist Church at Linwood and Park together with the Methodist church next door had a summer program that included some woodworking; they even had a jigsaw and we could make puzzles.

During the week it was scrub baseball at a lot at 39th and Olive. Calvin Keen was always the hardest man to put out. Or we'd go to Donnie Pope's house for Monopoly. His folks had an electric refrigerator with a coil on top. It would be some time before we had a refrigerator, and it came with a meter box that required quarters to make it run. Some evenings Herbie Baker's folks would include me for a trip to Swope Park, where we would lie on cots and watch the stars and wake up to a cool morning.

The Crown Drug Store at 39th and Prospect offered the chance now and then to be a delivery boy from 6 p.m. to midnight, for 50 cents plus tips, which sometimes amounted to a dollar or more. And

then there was the bowling alley across 39th Street that needed pin setters in the afternoons sometimes. If pin setting slowed and the snooker table was busy, there was always a chance of a tip for brushing off the felt top. Fridays were good days to work there; that was spiced shrimp night, and sometimes there would be some to share.

The Harris and Combs grocery at 34th and Park ran an account for our family that Mom tried to pay each payday. The store put out flyers for its weekly specials; we delivered the flyers door to door between Linwood and 39th Street from Michigan to South Benton. That was 50 cents you could count on.

We all had graduated from Horace Mann Elementary at 39th and Garfield and would be heading to Central Junior, which was a long way from our neighborhood. It would be some time later that this period of life would be known as hard times, but for then, as they say, "it was as good as it gets."

Published on July 13, 1997

Ice cream

By Steve White

Cherry-dip ice-cream cones — there's nothing else like 'em. But they must be from your neighborhood ice-cream stand. The kind where you walk up to the sliding screen window and order. Cold stuff from your grocer's freezer or even so-called ice-cream stores won't do. Nope, this is one area with no room for negotiation. I'll take one cherry-dip, please.

Growing up in Blue Springs, we had a fine ice-cream stand called Kremy Kones. Back in those days, my hometown's biggest claim to fame was two stoplights on a two-lane highway. Now it's known as one of the better suburbs of the Kansas City area, and it leaves me wondering if there's still a good place to get my cherry-dip cone.

I wonder because now I reside 500 miles east of Blue Springs. And Kremy Kones, unfortunately, became a casualty of suburban progress. For the last nine years, an unattractive strip mall has cluttered the landscape where our beloved Kremy Kones once held court in '50s-style, flat-roof grace.

"SHAKES MALTS SUNDAES ICE CREAM FLOATS" were the words adorning the tiny, chalk-colored shop. It was right off Highway 40, just a short jog down from the United Super where my big brother got to ride his bike to buy bread and where he once was blessed with a free can of Grape Nehi from the machine. (It is a child's duty to inspect every pop machine by furiously slapping all the panels in hopes of a freebie.) My folks took us to Kremy Kones during the drippy months of summer in Missouri. We'd go, oh, about once every three or four weeks. I never once got anything besides a cherry-dip. Unless you were a particularly quick ice-cream eater, you ended up with quite a few gooey drips down your little fingers on those humid evenings. Of course, the grown-ups were a tad smarter than we were — they used napkins.

And they had the sense to avoid what many people call "brain freeze," that is, eating ice cream so fast it causes a freezing sensation in your head. It borders on painful but more often is simply a silly feeling. One that causes the brain freezee to announce the event with muted pride and a little giggle.

Toward my adolescent years, my family occasionally visited Kremy Kones when we all happened to be home at once. But of course for us teen-agers, it just wasn't cool to be seen with your folks, let alone with nerdy brothers and sisters.

Those Kremy Kones days will forever remain in my heart. And though that venerable ice-cream stand stands no more, I have discovered solace in my travels. I enjoyed the rapture of flavor from a genuine cherry-dip cone last summer at my newfound neighborhood ice-cream stand — complete with sliding screen window.

One cherry-dip, please. And thanks for the memories.

Illustration by Lisa Morgan

Unless you were a particularly quick ice-cream eater, you ended up with quite a few gooey drips down your little fingers on those humid evenings.

Independence, 1948, West Lexington Street on the south side of the courthouse square.

Published on July 5, 1998

Independence Square

By Mary Jo Spake

When I attended William Chrisman High, 1937-41, Chrisman didn't have a cafeteria. Students could either go home for lunch, bring it, or buy it uptown. My girlfriends and I chose to go uptown.

During the school year, Independence Square became a hangout for teens because it was where many of us bought our lunch. We could get a meal for 25 cents at Woolworth or Crown Drug. An hour gave us time to eat lunch, window shop and catch up on the latest school gossip.

Uptown was a favorite meeting place for young and old and where everyone enjoyed circling the courthouse square.

The most popular reason for circling the square was a wedding procession. Numerous vehicles followed the bride and groom's car around the square. Cans rattled while horns blared. Pedestrians shouted and waved.

Supposedly cars weren't considered properly broken-in until they circled the square.

Business was good, so on-the-square parking was rarely available. Diehards often circled the square for 30 minutes before parking elsewhere.

Circling was certainly good for the ego, too. On his 16th birthday, my husband took his Model T Ford for a spin around the square.

Sometimes we met Sen. Harry S Truman (our classmate Margaret's father) walking around the square, laughing, talking and shaking hands with everybody.

Spontaneous circling usually happened after graduations, proms and victorious Chrisman homecoming games.

My business education began when Woolworth gave me my first job, working part time during the 1940 summer vacation.

That fall, Independence celebrated its heritage by staging the first Santa-Cali-Gon festival. Thousands cheered as horse-drawn carriages circled the courthouse square.

I graduated in 1941 and went to work at Grinter's Photography Studio on the north side of the square, over what is now a parking lot.

The square was preparing for Christmas when Pearl Harbor happened and changed our lives forever. The USS Arizona sank, taking Raymond Necessary with her. The class of 1941 mourned the loss of our friend and former classmate.

In 1942, I accepted a civil-service job in our nation's capital, making photostatic copies of papers.

With mixed emotions, I said farewell to friends and benefactors around the square. Saying goodbye to my family was something else.

I got lost my first day in Washington — going around the Dupont Circle. How embarrassing! I still laugh about that.

Just maybe the younger generations will continue to circle the Independence Square — for old times' sake.

Published on April 30, 2000

Indian Head Root Beer Stand

By Bob Goethe

The Indian Head Root Beer Stand, once near 36th and State in Kansas City, Kan.

Before McDonald's, before Burger King, before Hardee's, there was the Indian Head Root Beer Stand. It was a unique landmark, an oasis where you could quench your thirst and fill your stomach.

Located in the general area of 36th and State in Kansas City, Kan., it was the place to be on a hot summer night.

In 1953 Bob and Tom Waters bought the Big Chief from Morris Staton, a KCK fireman. The brothers worked the stand along with their wives and a bevy of carhops. Most of the carhops were energetic young ladies from the local high schools, always willing to work hard and to fill in for others. Orders were placed and picked up at windows that were in the Big Chief's mouth, kind of like movable teeth.

The quarters were cramped to say the least, with room for not much else other than the steam table and a couple of sinks. The inside was round with only an approximate 5-foot-diameter working area.

You had your choice of a hot dog, chili burger or Chief burger (soft style). All were served on hot-dog buns. To wash it all down, you could order the grape or orange drink (family recipes), a root beer or a root-beer float. Drinks were a dime for a large and a nickel for a small. There were free baby drinks, and, of course, all drinks were served in a mug.

Big Chief operated most of the year but closed during the winter months. With encouragement from loyal customers, the "Log Cabin" addition was built for winter business in 1953.

Unfortunately, winter business wasn't there, and the Log Cabin was moved to 75th and Leavenworth Road in 1954.

One time, part of the Indian Head — made of concrete — came crashing down on its own. Fortunately, the damage happened while the stand was closed, and no one was injured. The Waters were able to locate a versatile tradesman to make the reconstruction. The Indian Head Root Beer Stand was saved, at least that time.

I wish it were still there today. However, progress stops for no one, not even for the Indian Head Root Beer Stand. In about 1963, acres of land were purchased for what was going to be a grand-scale shopping center called Tower Plaza. The Big Chief had encountered his Waterloo.

Orders were placed and picked up at windows that were in the Big Chief's mouth, kind of like movable teeth.

Published on April 28, 1996

Junk cars

By Merle Sowell

My passenger-side window absolutely refused to roll down. With a desperation born of accumulated failures, I grabbed a good-sized rock and broke out the glass.

Like most drivers, I can vividly recall the thrill of purchasing my first car.

It was 1946. Used cars were hard to find after World War II. Someone told me there were lots of cars in Chicago, so I took my mustering-out pay from the U.S. Navy and bought a one-way bus ticket to the Windy City.

When the man at the used car lot offered to sell me a decrepit '35 Dodge for $375, I didn't even argue. I just handed over the cash.

No one had warned me that I should never, ever pay the first price that was quoted for a used car. I can just imagine how that salesman must have kicked himself for not asking more. A sucker like me couldn't have come along every day.

My heart was beating faster as I drove away and started down the long road back to Mountain Home, Ark. The front fenders were flapping like a gooney bird trying to take off, and the engine wasn't exactly purring. But the car was mine! All mine!

By Springfield, Ill., a rattle under the hood got too loud to be ignored. I pulled into a repair garage.

"You need new rod bearings," was the somber verdict. Next morning, I headed south again with my billfold $75 lighter and my heart heavier. Hey, these cars cost money.

It was only the beginning.

Two weeks after I got home, the brakes went out. Another $50 for repairs. In fact, each time I got one problem fixed on my prized car, another part would break down.

The headlights went out. Have you ever driven home in the dark, guided by a flashlight held out the window? It's not a journey for the faint of heart.

On a little joy ride, I started hearing a clatter from the engine. I tried to nurse the car home by slowing to 15 mph. But it was not to be. With a loud "bang!" the crankshaft broke. A tow truck was summoned.

One midsummer day, with the temperature hovering around 100 degrees in the shade, my passenger-side window absolutely refused to roll down. With a desperation born of accumulated failures, I grabbed a good-sized rock and broke out the glass. This had one unintended benefit: In rainstorms, my girlfriend had to sit right beside me to avoid getting wet.

I finally sold my old junker to a guy fresh from Oklahoma. I hope he's forgiven me somehow.

Illustration by Lisa Morgan

The Kansas City Power & Light Building, circa 1920-1930.

Published on February 8, 1998

Kansas City Power & Light Building

By Hazel E. Clevenger

The news in recent months about the Kansas City Power & Light Building and the changes proposed for the surrounding area have triggered fond memories of watching the lights magically change from one soft glow to another. I grew up in and around Kansas City in the 1920s and '30s with my mother and two sisters.

We frequently enjoyed the drive from Independence to Kansas City. Driving in our Model A Ford from Maywood on 15th Street (now Truman Road) to downtown, we enjoyed all the sights along the way. On the right was Mount Washington Cemetery and on the left close by was an old stone castle with a small lake and long curving drive like a scene from a fairy tale.

When we reached the stone arch bridge at Blue Ridge Boulevard, it made a perfect frame for a view of downtown and the new P&L Building. Then down the hill to cross the Blue River and wait for a steam engine and train to pass on the tracks in Centropolis. We thought it was big and scary but liked it when the engineer waved at us.

On the left was Manchester School, up the hill was the fire station, and a few blocks farther was the Aladdin Theater with its colorful tiles decorating the front. When we got to The Paseo, we could see a big sign atop the laundry building that proclaimed "Your Bosom Friend." That greatly embarrassed three little girls.

At 917 Grand Blvd., we had dancing lessons at Marie Kelley School of Dance, and mother had voice lessons with Ottley Cranston. I especially remember a soda fountain downstairs where we could get a large cherry or chocolate cola or a root beer for 5 cents.

In 1949, my husband and I and our two sons moved from Kansas City to our farm north of Orrick in Ray County. Recently I found on a shelf in the cellar a souvenir of the KCP&L company from about 1946, forgotten all these years. We had no electricity here until 1952 so this very interesting light fixture was never used again and no longer works. It was called a "Germ Kill Light." We bought it with a surcharge on our monthly bill. It is metal with a curved shiny reflector behind a long glass tube that issued an ultraviolet bluish light that was supposed to kill airborne germs.

I still wonder if it really killed germs.

Driving in our Model A Ford from Maywood on 15th Street (now Truman Road) to downtown, we enjoyed all the sights along the way.

Published on March 5, 2000

Katz Drug store: *the fire*

By William F. Welch

The Katz Drug store at Eighth and Grand, in 1923.

The Katz Drug store fire nearly cost six lives, including brother Byron's and mine.

It must have been about 1937, and the pharmacy chain had advertised a major pre-July 4 sale. We boarded the Northeast streetcar on Anderson at Bellefontaine and rode eagerly to our most convenient Katz store on Eighth at Grand Avenue. Our mission was to pick up a 25-cent cap pistol, a nickel box of caps and — oh, yes — a box of soap for Mother. Including carfare, the outing should have consumed exactly a dollar, except that we never bought the soap. Instead, the store went up in flames.

Years passed before anyone believed me, but the fire was deliberately started. Before I explain, consider the store's layout: Typical fire codes today do not permit any retail building to have just one doorway, yet the Katz doorway on the corner was the only way in or out of the store.

Also, today, few municipalities, if any, permit the retail sale of fireworks within city limits. There was no such restriction in Kansas City then. At Katz, three tables just inside the only door were filled nearly to overflowing with a wide variety of combustibles.

When we headed for the soap counter at the rear of the store, I saw a young man wearing a light gray business suit and broad-brimmed fedora spraying sparks from a toy machine gun onto a fireworks counter. I saw smoke curling up from the counter. Only a child, I simply did not recognize the danger and I scampered foolishly into the dead end of the store. Moments later, pandemonium erupted.

We were trapped: two children and four adults. Lying on our backs, we found smoky but breathable air until, perhaps 45 minutes later, a gigantic firefighter broke through to us. He led us into a storage basement

-– and ankle-deep black water — evidently thinking we would find a lower-level door on the building's north side. No. Builders had carved the basement out of the limestone that formed a backdrop to the White Castle Hamburger store on the corner at Seventh Street.

Firefighters eventually conquered the inferno, and the same giant led us safely to the outside. Everything within perhaps 25 feet of the door was shapeless black. We were lucky, so very lucky, to have survived.

We quietly crossed Eighth and took a streetcar home ... without the soap. Mother could have used it on our badly soiled clothing.

The Katz fire occupied only a paragraph in *The Kansas City Times*, but that blaze and others across the country did make a difference. Today, building and fire codes mandate precautions that nobody even considered then, surely saving lives.

I saw a young man wearing a light gray business suit and broad-brimmed fedora spraying sparks from a toy machine gun onto a fireworks counter.

Published on April 3, 1994

Kresge dime store

By Claudia Mundell

Shopping at the Kresge dime store, 1951.

*I*t was a festival of color, sound and smells. A trip through Kresge dime store was better than a trip to a zoo or a traveling carnival.

Large glass cases held bounties of chocolate, jelly beans, sugared orange slices and cinnamon hard candies. The aroma of freshly popped corn mingled with the syrupy sweet of the candies, making it hard for shoppers to leave the store without something edible in hand.

Beyond the candy counter were rows of necessary items such as Buster Brown T-shirts, silver tea balls, imitation crystal glasses at four for a dollar, curtain rods and days-of-the-week tea towels. Other aisles had even better prizes: rows of Tangee lipsticks in Flaming Orange and True Love Pink. Elegant cobalt blue bottles of Evening in Paris lay in cushioned boxes worthy of royalty.

But it was the far back corner of the store that always fascinated me. Racing across the once shiny hardwood floors, I headed for Pets. Blue and yellow parakeets chirped out competing

A trip through Kresge dime store was better than a trip to a zoo or a traveling carnival.

melodies, and multitudes of fish swam furiously in gigantic tanks complete with plastic greenery and ceramic divers.

One spring the Kresge menagerie had something new. In honor of Easter, it was selling baby chicks that were tinted pastel colors. They looked like an Easter rainbow of lavenders, mints and pinks.

I'll never know why my mother succumbed to the pleas of my sister and me. But that Easter we took home three baby chickens, and we named them Blue Bell, Yellow Bell and Pinkie. Dad built a small cage in the back yard to use when we weren't wrapping the chicks in doll blankets, pushing them in toy shopping carts or just hugging them.

Yellow Bell was the first catastrophe. One day we went outside to find only two of our feathered friends. Mother told us stories about predators such as wolves and foxes, but we eyed the neighbor's cat. We knew something had to be done.

Our grandmother lived on the

edge of town with a milk cow and a chicken coop made of strong, varmint-proof wire. Blue Bell and Pinkie went to live there. We visited often, but as their Easter colors faded, it became difficult to tell them from Grandma's hens.

On the Fourth of July that summer we had a big family reunion at Grandma's. When I tired of watching the men pitch horseshoes, I went to check out the progress of dinner. The women were setting out potato salad, sliced tomatoes and my favorite, fried chicken. It was then that I overheard Grandma telling Mother that she had dressed the spring chickens — including our two Easter chicks.

I went back outside and cried awhile by Grandma's chicken coop. I didn't eat my favorite dish that day for fear of eating my own Blue Bell or Pinkie. Eventually I would eat fried chicken again, and I continued to enjoy my adventures shopping at the Five-and-Dime. But I never again asked for an Easter chick from the Kresge store.

The Kresge dime store at 12th and Main, in 1951.

Mrs. El Mehdi Ben Aboud, the wife of the Moroccan ambassador, cuts the cake during Liberty Memorial rededication ceremonies in 1961, while Harry S Truman looks on.

Published on October 26, 1997

Liberty Memorial

By Jay Robert Jennings II

I do not recall any glamorous women in the rededication parade, but there were plenty of marching bands and uniforms.

Whenever you clean out the attic, you are bound to find something that conjures up a lost memory. This happened when I was up in the attic recently and found an American flag about 8 inches by 10 inches. I had not seen it in years, but I remembered it was the flag my mother had bought for me to wave when my father was in the parade for the November 1961 rededication of the Liberty Memorial. At that time, my father was a lieutenant colonel in a local A my Rese ve uni t and he was chosen to escort the ambassador of Ethiopia.

So we could see my father in the parade, my mother and I were on a knoll overlooking where Grand Avenue and Main Street now merge on the hill south of Union Station. Before the parade, my mother told me what she had seen at the dedication ceremony 40 years earlier.

She remembered sitting on her father's shoulders and seeing Queen Marie of Romania. Mom thought she had seen "the most glamorous woman in the world."

I do not recall any glamorous women in the rededication parade, but there were plenty of marching bands and uniforms. Even some World War I veterans were wearing their uniforms complete with flat helmets and wrap puttees.

There were two VIPs in the parade: Harry S Truman and Dwight D. Eisenhower. Mr. Truman was riding in a vintage, open car. ("That was General Pershing's staff car," Mom said.) "Captain Harry of Battery D" beamed while waving his hat to the cheering crowd. General Eisenhower soon appeared sitting atop the back of a Cadillac convertible. He was waving his arms and grinning just like he appeared in the newsreels of the World War II victory parades.

I was very impressed seeing two ex-presidents, but I was really trying to see my father. I had a flag to wave as he passed by and I did not want to miss him. After a while, there was a long break between the units in the parade. Then I saw an olive-drab Chevrolet coming up the parade route at a high rate of speed. As it passed by my vantage point, I saw my father sitting in the back seat of an Army staff car. The car went by so fast I could wave my flag only once. I was really put out.

Later that day, my father explained that he waited until the last possible minute for the ambassador of Ethiopia to arrive, but he did not show up. Finally, Dad was told by parade officials to join the parade and catch up. My father lost his chance to socialize in the world of diplomacy. But I saw one of the last events commemorating the war whose end was called Armistice Day.

Published on January 28, 2001

Loew's Midland Theatre

By Harma Petersen McKenzie

Loew's Midland Theatre, in 1927.

*T*here were four of us: black-haired Liz, auburn-haired LaVerne, "brownette" Johnnie and blond me. We met at the red brick station in Olathe to take the Strang Line electric streetcar to Kansas City. We chattered and giggled the whole way.

It was a beautiful Saturday, and our long-anticipated trip had become a reality. We were going to Loew's Midland Theatre to see Clark Gable in "Gone With the Wind."

First we went to the Forum Cafeteria for lunch. We were young high school girls who felt very grown-up as we made our food choices and paid our own checks.

Then we walked down to the theater in time for the afternoon matinee. We were awed at the lobby, with its magnificent long staircases and gorgeous crystal chandeliers. The ladies room, with huge mirrors and marble sinks, was impressive, too.

We sat in the balcony. The lights dimmed, and for the next four hours we were caught up in Margaret Mitchell's marvelous epic of the South. The introductory music of the theme from Tara stirred us as the wide screen showed the beginning scene.

We laughed and cried. It was a "three handkerchief" movie! We cried over Ellen's and Bonnie Blue's deaths. We sobbed when Rhett left. We laughed when Scarlett danced at the Confederate benefit ball and when she dressed in the green velvet curtains.

On our way home we had lots to talk about. We were enraptured with Rhett, who was handsome and daring. We were a little amused and shocked when he said "damn." It was the first time we'd heard that in a movie. (Sixty years later, it would seem mild.)

We thought Scarlett was beautiful and clever. Melanie was too sweet to be true, and Ashley was a "drip." Would Rhett ever return to Scarlett? It was our consensus that he would.

After that day we never did anything as a foursome again. We all graduated from St. John Memorial High School in Olathe. We went our separate ways to college and jobs. We married: a lawyer, a career military man, a chiropractor, a college professor. Our marriages each lasted 50 years-plus. We all traveled over the United States and overseas.

We seldom saw each other after graduation.

But that halcyon day in 1940 is a cherished memory of my youth.

We laughed and cried. It was a "three handkerchief" movie!

Clark Gable and Vivien Leigh wowed moviegoers in "Gone With the Wind."

Loose Park in 1945.

Published on August 24, 1997

Loose Park

By Kevin McShane

My first memories of Loose Park were of family picnics and the ducks. I don't remember how we got to Loose Park for sure the first time; we owned a car, but Mom didn't know how to drive in the 1940s, and my dad was in the Navy on the USS Iowa in the Pacific during World War II.

Most probably we took the streetcar to 55th and Brookside and walked over.

Our picnics included my mom, my brother, Denny, my sister, Sheila, and my cousin Jimmy Taylor. Our objective was to see the ducks. Each of us had a big loaf of white bread, and before we went the anticipation was high.

The gentle quacking ducks performed acrobatics individual to each duck. Baby ducks hovered near their mothers but tried to get any morsel of bread thrown within their reach. My mom sat back from the water on a bench because she didn't swim, but she encouraged us all to have a good time. As our group romped up and down the edge of the pond, we even forgot about being hungry ourselves. But when the bread ran out, we soon discovered the picnic basket filled with cookies, sandwiches, fruit and homemade lemonade.

The ritual of these picnics continued from late spring to early fall. Mom never had to ask twice if we wanted to go.

One time I slipped into the pond, and Denny jumped in, pulled me out and gave me artificial respiration. He was a Boy Scout and had special training for that type of water emergency. Even though I was young, I understood what he had done for me; we always had a special bond between us from that near-drowning. No one remembers clearly how old I was, but they do remember his jump into the murky water and the rescue.

Everyone loved the park, the ducks and the fun of the picnics. We returned many times, even after my dad came home from the war. In fact, he brought home a yellow life raft, and Jimmy Taylor and Denny launched the raft in the duck pond while we all cheered from the shore.

The ducks didn't come near this naval operation because we were so noisy, and I'm sure the yellow raft frightened them off — for the day at least. (The park department had a sign posted against boats and rafts, but we ignored this warning.)

Shortly after one of my birthdays, we returned to Loose Park to test two sailboats I received from friends and relatives. Each one had a metal ring on the back to secure twine, so if it tipped over, the sailboat wasn't lost. They glided with grace, while my family and I watched the movement of each one. There were also some battery-powered motorboats that other kids had, but they went in a straight line. The ducks were curious about the sailboats.

My memories as a teen-ager involved long walks beside the duck pond with girlfriends on sultry summer days. Later as an adult I took my own kids to the park for picnics, summer theater under the stars and feeding the ducks. Now it is a haven for me, a place to relax and "get my head together." While it certainly is not a Walden Pond, it serves the community with a tranquil setting in an urban background.

Published on April 16, 2000

Memorial Hall

By Alice Spickard

Flamboyant Gorgeous George (Wagner) grew his hair long, dyed it blond, then pinned it back with gold-plated bobby pins during his heyday, the 1940s to the early 1960s.

*L*iving in Trenton, Mo., I dreamed of the big city. At 16, I knew Kansas City was where I wanted to go. I left with only $4. A nice man who drove a produce truck to the City Market let me ride with him, and a friend then took me to find a room. The elderly couple who ran a boarding house at 12th and Shawnee in Kansas City, Kan., wanted $3 for the room but let me have it for $2 a week. That left me only $2. No food, for I chose to get a perm with the $2.

Off I walked on Kansas Avenue looking for work. A cafe named The Nite Hawk already had a cook and two waitresses. That seemed to be enough for the little cafe, so I went on by. I walked to the corner of Seventh Street and a little voice inside said "go back," so I did. The proprietor hired me to work at night. He paid me $1 a night, and that was for seven nights. His name was Harry, and soon he decided to put me on days so he could ask me to go to the wrestling matches at Memorial Hall. Three nights a week found us watching Gorgeous George be mean. The Forum Cafeteria on Main was another spot we went and then to the Midland Theatre. Never had I seen such a beautiful theater. I had stars in my eyes.

I married Harry, and we had three children. We sold the cafe and went to Missouri, where Harry worked as a chef for the Alcazar Hotel. There is so much more to our life in Kansas City.

Three nights a week found us watching Gorgeous George be mean.

Published on April 18, 1999

Metcalf South Shopping Center

By Laurie Barnes

Metcalf South Shopping Center in 1967.

In 1967 my world centered primarily on Antioch grade school on 75th Street and St. Mark's Methodist Church. From time to time I would venture into other parts of the city for special occasions — my 10th birthday dinner at Plaza III, for instance, and the fifth-grade field trip to the American Royal. However, life was mostly checking out books at the Antioch library and Saturday nights at the A&W for nickel root beers. It was, therefore, a thrilling moment when I learned that I would soon be going with my parents to an uncharted part of Kansas City: the new Metcalf South Shopping Center — to see a movie.

As we drove from 72nd and Antioch to 95th and Metcalf, it seemed as if we were traveling to the end of the world. Much like the 15th-century explorers who feared falling off the edge of the world if they ventured too far, I viewed our expedition as an adventure tinged with apprehension of the unknown.

Metcalf South seemed to be out in the middle of nowhere. I cannot honestly remember if there were buildings on the southwest and northwest corners of 95th and Metcalf, but I think there were only fields. How odd, I thought, to build such a new building so far out in the country! I don't think I'd ever been to a shopping mall before.

Naturally, at that time, Oak Park Mall and Mission Center didn't exist. My parents may have taken me at some point to the Ward Parkway mall, but I know for a fact I had never seen a movie inside a mall. I actually hadn't seen very many movies in my (relatively) short life. Moviegoing, like eating out, was a rare treat saved for special occasions. The movie we saw at Metcalf South that day was "Darby O'Gill and the Little People." The movie seemed to me to be one of unending enchantment and delight.

Thirty-one years later my family checked "Darby O'Gill" out of the library. The children, used to the advanced technology of the 1990s, laughed at some of the 1967 technology that tried to make regular-size actors look like leprechauns.

But my enjoyment of the movie the second time around was unmarred. As I watched I remembered the sheer excitement of going to a movie in a shopping mall way out in the middle of nowhere.

Metcalf South seemed to be out in the middle of nowhere.

Milgram's lady

By Karen Wilson

"Hi, neighbor!" It's Janie Fopeano, the Milgram's lady.

In the early days of my senior year at Park Hill High School, the girls were all abuzz over a new, black-haired sophomore boy whom I did not yet know. I wasn't at all sure what all the fuss was about. When I asked around, I just got giggles and answers like, "It's Peter Fopeano!" What that meant was a mystery to me, but not wanting to seem out of it or uncool in any way, I would smile knowingly and respond, "Ooooooh!" — like I knew what they were talking about.

After a few days of covert questioning I uncovered the next layer of the mystery: Peter was Janie Fopeano's son. Once again I played all-knowing and smiled appropriately, still no closer to my answer than before.

Finally, someone relieved my agony by telling me that Janie Fopeano had been the Milgram's lady, known for her cheery "Hi, neighbor!" greeting.

Memories flooded my mind. I remember being a little girl and visiting my grandmother in Independence. She, and all the ladies who were anybody, shopped exclusively at Milgram's. I remember when Grandma would take me shopping after finishing her morning school bus route. Everywhere we went we saw the face of the Milgram's lady: on billboards, on the sides of buses, on TV and, of course, everywhere we looked in the store. Some of my fondest childhood memories center on these shopping excursions with my grandmother and the Milgram's lady.

Janie, as the Milgram's lady, stood for womanhood, motherhood and apple pie. She symbolized the role that women held then. There was no apology for being a mother or a grocery shopper. She was as clean and wholesome as a mountain stream, and throughout the 1970s her smile galvanized women into action.

And then came that day in 1981 in that hallway at Park Hill High. Never in my wildest dreams as a child had I ever imagined that the Milgram's lady was actually a real person or that I would attend high school with her son and eventually meet the lady herself.

The Milgram's pitchwoman is just a memory now, a long-forgotten marketing strategy, as forgotten as the grocery chain itself. But for me she will always be linked with the memories of my now-deceased grandmother. Janie stood for the good and decent in the world. There seemed to be a lot more of that back then.

Janie, as the Milgram's lady, stood for womanhood, motherhood and apple pie.

Hemlines inching up in 1969.

Published on September 17, 1995

Miniskirts

By Robin A. Stiles

Her idea of what was "short enough" did not mesh with mine.

When I went to high school in the early 1970s, wearing a miniskirt was an art requiring expertise and cunning — only the truly practiced survived.

It was during this time I perfected two skills necessary to wear a miniskirt successfully: the drinking-fountain knee bend and the two-handed skirt stretch.

In executing the knee bend, I would approach the drinking fountain and bend from the knees, being careful to keep the back straight, and somehow still manage to get a drink. The maneuver was further complicated if the mini-wearer had long hair; then she had to add the extra procedure of holding back the hair while straightening, bending and drinking.

The second skill, the two-handed skirt stretch, was only used when climbing stairs. To do this, I held the bottom of my skirt at each side, pulling until there was no gap between the skirt and my legs. (If you couldn't reach the bottom of your skirt, it was too long.) Of course, holding your skirt in such a manner made climbing the stairs a little tricky, but with practice, it could be achieved.

This maneuver, however, depended on one of two factors: Either I had no books to carry, or someone (preferably a boy) carried them for me. If neither factor was an option, I could always opt for the single-handed skirt stretch, but this move was not recommended for novices.

Before I could put any of my miniskirt-wearing techniques into practice, I had to get past the scrutinizing eye of my mother. Her idea of what was "short enough" did not mesh with mine. To get around this potential problem, I would leave the house with my skirt at a length acceptable to Mom. When I got to school, I would rush to the bathroom and roll or pull until the skirt was at a length acceptable to me. On the way home, I would reverse the procedure, and everyone was happy.

Oh yes. One vital mini-wearing skill I forgot to mention — the art of sitting in a mini. That would take entirely too much time to explain here, and would require diagrams. Suffice it to say that I stood as much as possible.

Minnesota Avenue in 1951.

Published on September 20, 1998

Minnesota Avenue

By Sherry Bishop

The area on Minnesota Avenue between Fifth and 10th was a hubbub of activity.

If you lived in Wyandotte County during the years following World War II, that is, the late 1940s, the only place to be on Saturday night was "on the Avenue."

What a fun and glorious time was had by all who congregated there. The area on Minnesota Avenue between Fifth and 10th was a hubbub of activity. Believe it or not, the stores stayed open until 9 p.m.!

Many came early to eat at Thomas' Cafeteria or the Blue Willow Restaurant before meandering back and forth on both sides of the street. Often, families would venture one block north to Meyer's Ice Cream Store for the best, thickest malts in Greater Kansas City. The waitress would fill your glass with the yummy malt, then give you the rest in the mixing container.

There were two big drugstores, Katz and Crown, located a block apart. They each had a soda fountain where you could get a cherry phosphate or chocolate Coke, while you sat with your friends in booths at Katz, or on stools at Crown.

On the corner of Sixth and Minnesota, Kresge had a coffee shop that was the length of the store on the east side. It was always full, and people waited to grab a stool as soon as one was vacated.

There was another dime store, McClellen's, in the same block. Penney's, Montgomery Ward and locally owned Young's had large stores that kept Kansas shoppers in Wyandotte County. Plus, many specialty stores for women, such as Leader, Maslin's and Bodker's offered great selections of apparel. Two jewelry stores, Helzberg's and Goldman's, took care of those necessities. Another place that got a lot of attention was called "The Store Without a Name." It was on the corner at Seventh and Minnesota.

Nor were we without movie theaters. There were three on the Avenue within blocks of one another. One of them, the Electric, even had amateur nights on some Saturday evenings. This was many years before videotapes and discs. If you were interested in buying a record, you asked the clerk to play a little of it on a phonograph (sorry kids) and you then decided whether you wanted it. You could buy sheet music at the same counter.

One Saturday evening, my cousin and I had them play a record for us, and we did an impromptu dance right in front of the counter. My uncle was mortified, but the onlookers clapped along with the music, and two other folks joined us as we twirled around.

In those days it was all good, clean fun.

The Royal Theater at 1022-24 Main.

Published on November 2, 1997

Movie theaters

By Lee Marts

*For that dime we usually saw a cartoon,
newsreel, short comedy and a feature film
— sometimes a double feature.*

Recent publicity about the proposed "Centertainment District" plan stirs wonderful memories of Downtown Kansas City during the 1930s and 1940s, when the area was saturated with movie theaters.

Along Main Street from 11th to 14th streets were the first-run houses — the Paramount, Loew's Midland and the Mainstreet — and at 12th and McGee was the Pantages (later the Tower Theatre). But there were also numerous "B" picture and second-run houses, like the Liberty and the Royal on Main, and the Regent and Downtown on 12th between Walnut and Grand, as well as the Empire, the Globe and others.

My brother and I grew up between 14th and 16th on Broadway. Almost every week we managed to wheedle a dime apiece for a Saturday or Sunday movie from Grandma, who raised us. For that dime we usually saw a cartoon, newsreel, short comedy and a feature film — sometimes a double feature.

The Tower and the Mainstreet also had vaudeville performances, in addition to movies, and we got to see some of the country's leading performers: Sammy Davis Jr., Red Skelton, Bert Lahr, Joe E. Lewis, Sophie Tucker, Sally Rand. Those were only a few of the big-name performers who appeared in Kansas City. Plus there were the singers, dancers, acrobats, musicians and comedians who completed the bills. All this and a first-run movie. Sometimes we sat through two shows — on the front row, if we got there early enough.

When we became teen-agers we had to pay adult admission, 25 cents at the major theaters.

By this time we had part-time jobs and sometimes could afford to take dates to the movies. It was very impressive to walk through the ornate lobbies or to sit in the beautifully decorated lounges while waiting for the beginning of the next feature. (There may have been some hand-holding, but don't believe those stories that we only sat in the balcony.) We didn't realize it at the time, but we were experiencing cinematic history. We saw first releases of film classics "Lost Horizon," "The Good Earth," "Casablanca," "Frankenstein" and many others.

All this was Downtown Kansas City from the Depression years up to World War II. It was a wonderful and exciting place to grow up. It will never be duplicated, but it would be great to see the area rejuvenated for the enjoyment of new generations.

Municipal Auditorium

By Claudia Mundell

The cast of the Ice Capades, in 1941.

*The performance
was better than
anything we could
have imagined.*

A trip to "The City" was always a special treat. My family lived in Warrensburg, Mo., and for special occasions we would drive the 50 miles to Kansas City. One such outing was in the late 1940s.

My cousin John and I had been given tickets to the Ice Capades at Municipal Auditorium in downtown Kansas City. John was 10 years old, and I was 8, and we were on our own. That is, my mother and aunt dropped us off in front of the marquee and we were to meet them after the performance in the lobby of the Muehlebach Hotel.

Dressed in our best outfits, we were ushered to our seats. The performance was better than anything we could have imagined. The skaters sailed over the ice in glittering costumes. They jumped in the air, twirled and performed unbelievable feats. John and I sat on the edge of our seats. ... And then it was over! We were so disappointed; it had been so short.

We left the grand marble halls and walked the three blocks to the Muehlebach. Once in the lobby, we sat and sat. Finally my mother and aunt arrived and inquired how long had we been waiting. After telling them we had been there for an hour, they exclaimed: "You left at the intermission!"

How were two kids from Warrensburg supposed to know about intermissions?

Municipal Stadium in 1960.

Published on June 17, 2001

Municipal Stadium

By Michael Perkins

The pinch-hit single by Don Bollweg that broke open the A's initial game in the sixth inning, in Municipal Stadium, in April 1955.

I can still see that ball bouncing in the street so high that I thought it would jump onto the rooftops of the houses on the east side of the street.

I drove by the site of the old Kansas City Municipal Stadium the other day. The small, vacant lot that is there now certainly could not have held such a giant stadium.

In 1954 I went to my first game at old Municipal Stadium. The Kansas City Blues played there then. But my real memories of how big the stadium was came when the Philadelphia Athletics moved to town and became the Kansas City A's.

Going to the stadium for a ball game was quite an adventure for a 9-year-old kid from the suburbs who hadn't spent much time in the city. We usually parked in someone's front yard about a block from the ballpark. There'd be a sign in the yard that read AUTO PARK. My dad would hand over a couple of dollars, and we'd head for the stadium.

I can still remember the smell when you first walked in — hot dogs and popcorn mixed with the distinct odor of cigar smoke. The old men would be sitting in the back rows of the lower deck in their white shirts with their sleeveless undershirts showing through. And every one of them, it seemed, would be smoking something: Lucky Strikes, cigars or the occasional pipe.

But then you looked out on the field. It was so big, and the grass so green, especially at night, when the huge light towers cast bright yellow all over the field. The fences seemed so far away, and the big Schlitz Beer scoreboard looked enormous.

But those fences didn't seem so far away the day Larry Doby of the Cleveland Indians hit one out on Brooklyn Avenue. I can still see that ball bouncing in the street so high that I thought it would jump onto the rooftops of the houses on the east side of the street. That's where the people would come out and watch the games from the rooftops, much like Chicago's Wrigley Field neighbors.

I remember Sam's Parking Lot out beyond left field being bigger, too. Yet when I went by recently, you couldn't even imagine a baseball field being there with a huge parking lot just north of it. I can still see Kansas City's Gus Zurnial hitting a homer that flew out into that parking lot. How I laughed when I heard someone's car getting hit with the ball. I sure wouldn't laugh today if my car got hit like that.

But when you're a kid, you see things differently, like the greatness of an old stadium and the wonderful memories of that time. The players, the field and the experiences seemed larger than life back then.

Oh, how I'd like to spend just one more afternoon sitting with my dad watching the A's play the Indians at old Municipal Stadium.

Hey Dad, who's up next?

Published on April 11, 1999

Music Hall

By Allan M. Hurst

Children watching a performance in Music Hall, circa 1950.

Attending grade school in the 1940s in the Kansas City school system meant getting a thorough grounding in the arts, as well as academic subjects.

The teachers I had at McCoy School spent a great deal of time preparing us for visits to both the Nelson-Atkins Art Museum and the Kansas City Philharmonic. Music taught on the old Victrola by our seventh-grade teacher, Miss Boarman, was pointed toward one of the highlights of the school year: the visit to a performance of the Philharmonic.

After learning the basics of the music to be featured, with the requisite sorties into elementary form and tone color, the class was loaded onto a bus and transported downtown to the Music Hall, itself a wonder to young and impressionable youth. Built in the 1930s, the Music Hall was still quite new. With its shining marble floors, gilt inlaid decorations, copious murals and plush seats, it had the splendid air of a potentate's palace.

We filed into the performance hall, along with hundreds of other kids from all over the city, and waited in what I remember as almost reverent silence as the black-clad musicians walked out on the stage. At the appointed time, and after the tuning of the instruments, the auditorium dropped into silence again. After a dramatic pause, the conductor appeared from offstage and threaded his way through the waiting orchestra to the side of the podium. All of us had been drilled in the protocol of concert behavior, so we knew what came next.

As the conductor approached the podium and bowed his lanky frame, a chorus of applause rose from the audience, too long kept in restraint. The spectacle of all the musicians dressed so fine was powerful, and the addition of one so obviously important and skilled evoked a rising swell of clapping, which diminished only as he turned and stepped upon the dais to face his orchestra. He waited for complete silence in the vast hall before he launched himself into the first selection.

The conductor was Maestro Efrem Kurtz, a storklike creature who waved, stabbed and thrust his baton at the orchestra. He sometimes stood on one leg in a precarious blancing act at the very edge of the podium, shaping and fashioning the music, which came forth in glorious waves.

It was mesmerizing. The players seemed to respond in kind, although less theatrically, as the sound rose to great crescendos in the tutti passages. Dressed as he was in long tuxedo tails, Kurtz made a visual impact that was in keeping with the power of the music. My eyes drifted to the players from time to time, but the frenetic swordplay of the conductor demanded my attention. He was the central actor in the drama in front of us. It made a lasting impression.

My eyes drifted to the players from time to time, but the frenetic swordplay of the conductor demanded my attention.

Maestro Efrem Kurtz in 1947.

The Junior Gallery and its Indian Art at the Nelson-Atkins Art Museum, 1961.

Published on February 21, 1999

Nelson-Atkins Art Museum

By Dan Henry

Rozelle Court at the Nelson-Atkins Art Museum, 1934.

I had to be dragged away from the American Indian dioramas in the basement.

The Nelson art gallery had been open only two years. I had been on the planet only 10. Here's this naive kid from Coffeyville, Kan., whose previous travels seldom exceeded 40 miles from home, staring in awe at that gorgeous building and its grounds. I had no idea what was inside, but the exterior was far and away the most beautiful structure I'd ever seen.

Then we went in. Wow! How'd they do that?! Black marble columns that reached to the moon. An open courtyard with zodiac signs focusing on a huge fountain. Knights in armor astride eager chargers and glistening white marble statuary everywhere. "I don't think we're in Kansas anymore, Toto!"

I had to be dragged away from the American Indian dioramas in the basement. They were so realistic I just knew there was life in those figures, and I wanted to be there when one of them moved. Mother used to say, "It's impolite to stare and point," but Emily Post was left behind in Coffeyville. I stared at the miniatures for an eternity, gaped at that ceramic chandelier until my neck was cramped, dropped my jaw at the sight of that huge wooden gate in the Oriental room and marveled at the painted wooden figures and wall behind it. I pointed at ivory and jade cricket cages and just couldn't believe anyone could be so talented as to create that inlaid marble tabletop.

But even though I was surrounded by splendor and spectacle never before encountered, the memory of one painting is more vivid than any other. It's by a Dutch master. It's so detailed I still can't comprehend the skill involved. From a few feet away you see a nicely done bouquet, but step closer and the wonder of it all comes into focus: ants so realistic they seem to crawl, dew drops so liquid you expect them to run, bees and other insects, and the veins and colors in each flower petal so true to life you can detect their fragrance. Now that's art!

That first visit was in 1935. Counting the number of visits since would only provoke unwelcome thoughts of advancing years, and although the Nelson doesn't show its age, I can't say the same. However, there's one easy way for this old man to open the door to pleasant memories and feel like a 10-year-old kid again: Just visit the Nelson.

(Dan Henry is a retired WDAF-TV weatherman.)

Published on May 20, 2001

Nightclubs

By Ida Rose Luke Feingold

Reno Club, circa 1937. Bill Searcy on piano, Christyanna Buckner on vocals and Curtyse Foster on sax.

Nightclubs proliferated in the Kansas City area in the mid-1930s, and every weekend one could find the teen-age Luke Sisters advertised as star performers at one of these nightspots.

We were the Luke Sisters, Zelda and Rosida. I was Rosida. Well, not really. I was actually Ida Rose, but one of our booking agents thought my name to be nontheatrical and changed it to Rosida.

We were very popular because a sister team made a nice opening and closing for floor shows that came on at 11 p.m., 1 a.m. and 3 a.m. We'd open with a fast tap and close with a double acrobatic; in between we'd perform our solos. Zelda, advertised as a personality singer, performed tunes such as "Goody, Goody," "Stop, You're Breaking My Heart" and "You Can't Pull the Wool Over My Eyes." I did a tap dance while jumping rope or, later, using a wooden hoop. My crescendo at the end was wiggling it around like a Hula-Hoop, although Hula-Hoops hadn't been invented yet.

And what was our average pay? For one night we received $3 to $5, not each, but for the team. Mother, who usually accompanied us, was our manager, costume designer and seamstress. She bought a rhinestone-studding machine and produced sparkling, stunning outfits. There were no disc jockeys; orchestras and bands played for us.

When our five kids were grown, they wanted to see where their mommy had danced. They loved some of the names of the clubs: Sloppy Joes, Dante's Inferno, Cocked Hat. They were particularly intrigued by the Reno Club on East 12th, because I had told them that Count Basie and his band played for us there in 1938.

So in the 1960s I got the kids in the car to give them the grand tour and history of our dancing days. Lo and behold, the nightclubs were all gone.

The 85 Club, an upscale place at 85th and Wornall, had given way to Kiddieland; now it's a bank. Mary's Club at 8013 Wornall is now a building with a sign that says "Natural Choice." The Cocked Hat at 4151 Troost has been knocked down and is now an auto repair shop. What used to be Sloppy Joes at 3114 Gillham Plaza now houses a temporary labor enterprise.

In 1939 my sister and I worked our way East, making Chicago our last job before heading to New York for the World's Fair. We came home on Sept. 1 to the headline of HITLER INVADES POLAND in *The Kansas City Times*. War was at hand. Our professional dancing days were over.

Zelda, three years younger than I, would start college; I would start my teaching career. Memories of two young girls dancing the nights away, never missing a day of school, helping to contribute to the family's weakened income during those Depression years, will always be with me.

Those were the days, my friend, never to come again.

They were particularly intrigued by the Reno Club on East 12th, because I had told them that Count Basie and his band played for us there in 1938.

Baseball pitcher extraordinaire Satchel Paige.

Published on May 6, 2001

Paige, mud balls, windy streets

By Nola Laflin

I secured the autograph from this man with the longest fingers I'd ever seen.

I grew up in a house at 29th and Woodland that no longer stands. I attended schools that no longer exist.

The streetcar ran in front of our house. As children we labeled every streetcar with mud balls thrown from the curb. No matter what we were doing as a streetcar passed, all heads would turn to see if the marking was still visible. If not, mud balls would be made to hurl at the car as it passed on its return downtown.

There were no swimming pools nearby. When rain would start to pour on a hot summer day, all the kids in the neighborhood would hurriedly don their swimming suits. Wading in the water as it ran down the street next to the curbs was a cooling activity.

I remember St. Vincent's Catholic Church and school, where I attended. There I was taught the following verse:

Whenever you pass by a church,
Stop to make a visit.
So when you're carried in
The Lord won't say, "Who is it?"

I remember spooning with a beau on Scout Hill overlooking the magnificent Liberty Memorial and Union Station. One day I waited in a very long line for an autograph in Union Station because I saw everyone else doing it. After I secured the autograph from this man with the longest fingers I'd ever seen, I returned to my friends, who asked me who it was. I had to tell them I didn't know, but I thought the man — Satchel Paige — might be one of the Harlem Globetrotters.

I remember the thrills of a trip downtown. Legend had it that on windy downtown streets it was easy to tell the country girls from the city girls: The country girls held their skirts; the city girls held their hairdos.

I remember the Missouri Buffet bar and restaurant on 12th Street. It had a platter over the bar that read: "A wife who cooks and does the dishes should be granted these three wishes: a helpful mate, a kiss on the cheek and a restaurant meal every week." I've used that often.

I remember the magnificent Muehlebach Hotel, where I attended a beauty contest for the auto show in 1953. I was chosen Miss Buick. The real plus of the evening was when President Harry Truman came back to greet each of us and shake our hands after his private viewing of the cars.

I would have gone to college to pursue a career in writing, but I had to work two years before I was able to pay back my tuition for Bishop Lillis High School, which my mother could not afford, and then I married that beau from Scout Hill.

May all your memories be warm and fuzzy.

Published on August 13, 2000

Paseo Bridge

By John J. Sullivan

The Paseo Bridge, right after its opening in 1954.

The Paseo Bridge is looking a little tattered and sad these days and is in bad need of a coat of paint.

As a 21-year-old apprentice electrician in 1954, I worked for over a year on the Paseo Bridge project. The bridge was built by the American Bridge Co. and is Kansas City's only suspension bridge. The steel was all connected with hot rivets.

Many of the ironworkers who constructed the bridge were of Mohawk and Shinnecock Indian descent. Their ancestors built the great skyscrapers and bridges of New York City, including the Empire State Building, Rockefeller Center, the Chrysler Building and the Brooklyn, Williamsburg and Queensborough bridges.

After completing the Paseo Bridge, their next project was the great Mackinac Bridge across the Mackinac Straits in northern Michigan.

Many skilled ironworkers from Local Union No. 10 here in Kansas City also worked on the project.

It was really something to see the ironworkers heat, throw and catch the hot rivets at those great heights — an art and craft that I am not sure is still in existence.

All the construction crews took great pride in their work and the challenge of getting the job done over a fast-moving Missouri River some 150 feet below.

There were manned lifeboats stationed at each end of the project by the north and south piers in case someone fell. As near as I can remember, there were at least three serious accidents, and one man, a carpenter who was helping set forms for the concrete decks, fell and lost his life.

As our great city starts its 151st year, the city or state or whoever is responsible for the maintenance of the bridge should bring it back to life with a good coat of paint. Such a great, visible landmark deserves it.

It was really something to see the ironworkers heat, throw and catch the hot rivets at those great heights.

Children sledding in the street near 68th and Paseo, circa 1930s.

Published on December 31, 2000

Paseo snow

By Michael J. Ryan

Earlier this month Kansas City was struck with the largest snowfall in several years: Parts of the city received 8 to 11 inches. My wife and I, upon looking out the window, began reflecting on the winters of our childhood.

We still remember the excitement we'd feel upon awakening to a large snowfall — no school, and the wonder of the landscape. Over the breakfast table, we kids would plot out our "regular" snow-shoveling customers and plan the attack. We'd don endless layers of clothing, rubber galoshes (the ones with the impossible buckles), scarfs, stocking caps and socks on our hands (under our jersey gloves). Then we'd grab our shovels and go door-to-door asking to shovel neighbors' walks and drives. The going rate, as I recall, was $1, or $2 for an especially large area. After a morning of shoveling, we'd head home, warm up and plan the afternoon's fun.

On a winter afternoon, nothing was more pleasurable than meeting friends, pooling sleds and proceeding to the massively large and long hills on 42nd Street from Highland to Flora. Usually 8 to 12 of us would trudge up the two hills, hit the sleds and fly down. We'd post lookouts at each intersection to watch for cars. Should one be spotted, an arm would go up, there'd be a shout of "Car!" — and the sledders would steer to the curb to be abruptly stopped and dumped from the sled.

On a good run, we'd make it down both hills across the intersection at Flora Avenue and part of the way up the hill toward the Paseo. After several good runs, we'd proceed to the corner store owned by the mother and grandmother of one of our compatriots, to warm ourselves and dry our jersey gloves on the open gas heater in the middle of the store. The smell of jersey gloves steaming on that stove is still with me.

In the winter of 1958, we experienced one of the worst snowstorms in Kansas City's recorded weather history. Over two days, the area was blanketed with 18 inches of snow. The entire city came to a standstill — and we kids were absolutely in heaven. In those days, the Paseo was a major north-south thoroughfare for the city. In clearing the street, snowplows would literally bury numerous parked cars. Again, we kids would grab our shovels and end up making a pretty good wage digging out rows of parked cars along the Paseo. We'd dig all the snow from around the car and push the car and driver from the curb to get them on their way. Had it not been for our parents, we would not have come back home until every single car was rescued.

Today, sitting in our home, watching the snow fall, we remember the joy and excitement of a blanket of snow in a child's imagination. As adults, we take a somewhat dimmer view of the beautiful white stuff but are so lucky to have such delightful memories.

Published on December 27, 1998

Petticoat Lane

By Gloria Hoffman

Bustling Petticoat Lane, circa 1940s, looking east along 11th from Main.

_I_t was 1954, a very good year to remember.

In March I made my first visit to Kansas City, to meet the very large family of a young man I had dated while he was serving his two-year naval stint in my hometown of Norfolk, Va.

I flew on a Constellation to the downtown airport from Madison, Wis., where I was completing my senior year at the university. And I arrived here with a monstrous sinus-bronchial infection, not to mention a case of the nerves.

Several days later I returned to school half-well but newly engaged.

In June, right after graduation, I was whisked back to Kansas City on the train. This time there were china, crystal and silver patterns to select and bridal gowns to see. Kansas City was an un-cool 104 degrees.

But my dream wedding gown was waiting for me on Petticoat Lane. Blush pink peau-de-soie, pearl encrusted bodice, circular train snapping up into a peplum for post-wedding dancing. I called Daddy in Norfolk — collect.

The wedding was a gala event in Norfolk in mid-September. About 60 people came from Kansas City via planes and trains.

By October we were ensconced on the Plaza at the James Russell Lowell. I was notified of a really big family event coming up in November: the free Katz Philharmonic concert with Eddie Fisher as guest artist.

I was off to Petticoat Lane again, this time with my mother-in-law and my aunt, who had come down from Aurora, Ill. I selected a delft blue wool Ann Fogarty dress, classic leather opera pumps and purse, plush neutral hat and white kid gloves.

"The family" was the Katz family of Katz Drug Co. I had married Frank Katz Hoffman, Ike Katz's oldest grandchild.

We sat in a box at that concert. Afterward we walked to the old Muehlebach Hotel for a post-concert supper for members of the Philharmonic and their families and for Eddie Fisher and his fiancee, Debbie Reynolds.

My sisters-in-law will never let me forget what I blurted out to Debbie Reynolds — when at last I found the courage to speak: "Just be sure to keep up with your thank-you notes!"

But my dream wedding gown was waiting for me on Petticoat Lane.

Dancing at the Pla-Mor in the 1940s.

Published on October 15, 1995

Pla-Mor

By Jane Jones Aubrey

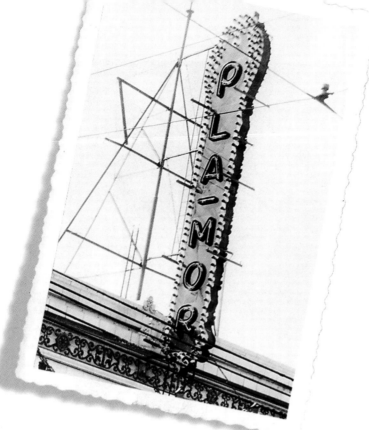

One of my happiest memories of those early days of World War II is my best friend and I as teen-agers, roller skating there every Friday night.

When I moved to Kansas City at age 12 in the early 1940s, one of the first places I heard about was the Pla-Mor. A great place for ice skating, roller skating, bowling, billiards and more.

The Pla-Mor, in the 3200 block of Main Street, was 4 acres of amusement and recreation, the largest such establishment under one roof when it was built in 1927.

One of my happiest memories of those early days of World War II is my best friend and I as teen-agers, roller skating there every Friday night. There was no worry then about a weight problem; we skated it off without even thinking about it.

On rare occasions we would bowl, then have a hamburger before going home. Such innocent pastimes.

One memory stands out after we started dating.

One New Year's Eve we were watching the clock. The lights began to dim at five minutes until midnight. By prearrangement my friend and I skated to the ladies' room, having heard that at midnight the lights would go out, everyone would start kissing and we would be expected to kiss our dates.

We stayed there until five after midnight, listening to "Auld Lang Syne," horns tooting, balloons popping and laugher.

Another time we tried to ice skate. After I fell, a tall, handsome Marine scooped me up rather disgustedly, as though I were a child and set me firmly on my feet out of the way of hundreds of flashing blades. I never ice skated again.

One night my friend's boy cousin from Boston was down for the weekend. After bowling we walked my friend home first and then he walked me home. He was very polite. I remember feeling grown-up for the first time. I was 16. He was old — 18 — and soon to be a Navy man fighting for our country.

Downtown began to change with the growth of suburbia. The ballroom closed in 1951, and the rest of the Pla-Mor a short time later.

Eastertime at the Plaza, circa 1970s.

Published on October 24, 1999

Plaza bunnies

By Vicki Shuster

We drove through downtown and then south toward a wonderful place called the Plaza.

Last summer, as I prepared to move to Wyoming, memories kept surfacing of my family's move to Kansas City 43 years ago from Fort Wayne, Ind.

My father, working as an advertising manager for Sears, had just accepted a transfer. Our imaginations ran amok: My mother, brother and I had visions of a dirty, flat cowtown full of gangsters and Wild West happenings! In an attempt to pique our interest and assure us that we were moving to a "modern and civil" city, Dad showed us a brochure photo of our new home, a modern design called a "split level" (painted turquoise, no less) in a newly developed suburb called "Prairie Village." Prairie Village? "Dad, you sure we won't be living in the wide open with cowboys?"

The best thing to do, Dad decided, was arrange for us to see Kansas City in person. During spring break we took a train trip, arriving at busy, bustling Union Station.

As soon as we got off the train, Dad whisked us across the street to see Liberty Memorial. We rode the elevator to the top, which was lighted by a 24-hour gas flame, and enjoyed a spectacular 360-degree view of sprawling Kansas City. Next, we drove through downtown and then south toward a wonderful place called the Plaza. It was our first glimpse of a "shopping center." It was Easter, and several large bunny statues with glowing red bulbs for eyes decorated the sidewalks. We delighted over the fountains throughout the area.

Next we visited beautiful Loose Park, admiring the lovely rose garden and landscaped pond full of swimming ducks. We drove down a wonderfully huge divided street called Ward Parkway; I squealed with delight as Dad sped around the traffic circle at Meyer Boulevard.

Our cowtown fantasy of Kansas City quickly vanished and was replaced by exciting reality as we visited Prairie Village, a new suburb full of brand-new houses; the new Somerset Elementary School, which I would attend; and Indian Hills Junior High, another new school that my brother would attend.

On that trip we stayed at the Riviera Hotel on the Plaza, and each day we walked on the "humped" bridge spanning Brush Creek to explore the many wonderful stores across the way.

Last summer, as we headed for Laramie, I couldn't help wondering what my new home would be like. Would it be a dirty, flat cowtown full of gangsters and Wild West happenings? Hmmm ...

Published on June 20, 1999

Plaza eateries

By Glen Enloe

Putsch's on the Plaza in 1971.

I had just gotten out of college and was still living in Warrensburg when I got word that I had been hired as an advertising copywriter for a real-estate company then known as United Farm Agency on the Country Club Plaza. This was it, I thought, the big time!

As those early years of the 1970s rolled by, I became acquainted with some of the area's more affordable eating establishments. One was Putsch's Cafeteria, with its somewhat 1950s air of conservative tastes and an older clientele. But it was always reasonably good, had great coffee and, most of all, was affordable on my still-small salary. Then there was the old Woolworth lunch counter, even then a fading relic of the past that still served up great apple and cream pies and piping-hot roast beef and turkey dinners. It wasn't gourmet, but it fit the bill and the budget.

There was also the now long-gone Plaza Bowl. It featured fresh grilled cheeseburgers and, my favorite, a terrific Reuben sandwich that I still have not been able to find the equal of anywhere. All this and the sound of exploding bowling pins in the background to enhance your dining experience!

My introduction to Chinese food on the Plaza was at the House of Toy. It boasted wonderful and reasonably priced lunchtime specials of chop suey, chow mein, eggrolls and hot tea. The old Putsch's Sidewalk Cafe and coffeehouse were less-frequented spots for me. Then there was the then-new Harry Starker's (great salads, bookbinder soup and waitresses), Houlihan's, 100 West (which later became Annie's Santa Fe), the Observatory and the Subway (downstairs in Woolf Brothers). Only a few blocks away was the Main Street Delicatessen and, a little farther away, the original site of Streetcar Named Desire, now in Crown Center.

Only a few months before the fateful Plaza flood of 1977, I started a new job in another state. About 15 years later, I rejoined the real-estate company, now named United Country Real Estate, at a new location on the far end of the Plaza. The first thing I did when I returned was check out my old haunts. Much to my dismay, most of them were either gone or had moved. I guess nothing ever stays the same, not even the places of our fondest memories.

It was always reasonably good, had great coffee and, most of all, was affordable on my still-small salary.

Published on December 14, 1997

Plaza lights

By B.T. "Teddy" Kelley

The Plaza lights in 1965, seen from near the J.C. Nichols fountain.
Note the absence of the Giralda Tower, which wouldn't be constructed until 1967.

In the mid to late 1940s, my father, mother, little brother and I lived on Etem's Dairy Farm in Hickman Mills. Daddy worked for the Etem Farm, and my mother was an employee of the newly built Sears store on the Plaza. She helped put the china department together and later transferred to the candy department.

My father wasn't too excited about driving into the city, which he considered the Plaza to be. But lo and behold, one Saturday afternoon he consented to take my brother and me to see where our mother worked and to visit her.

I felt so proud when I saw my mother behind that huge wrap-around counter strolling from one delicious morsel to another. I imagined myself being able to eat all the candies I could digest. Naturally that scenario never occurred. I had to settle for one small piece.

A few weeks after our visit to see Mother at work, it was Thanksgiving and time for the Plaza lights to be illuminated for the holiday season. I acquired this information from the local radio station.

I immediately began pondering a strategy to convince my father that this was a once-in-a-lifetime phenomenon for his children to observe and how much enjoyment it would also be for him.

Miracle of all miracles happened. After a few minutes "shedding of the tears" (my strategy), our little family piled into our '33 Ford and headed out into the darkness toward the Plaza.

Wornall Road was my favorite route to the city because of all the beautiful homes lining both sides of the street. I began choosing which houses I'd like to live in when I grew up.

As we topped the hill that overlooks the Plaza area, there, like magic, was a breathtaking array of bright, dazzling, twinkling colored lights adorning all the buildings. My wish to see the lights had come true.

I never did get to live in one of those homes along Wornall. But in the fall of 1979, Channel 5 and the Plaza Association sponsored a drawing of postcards sent in by residents who were interested in pushing the lever that would turn on the Plaza lights.

My daughter, Tracy, who was a junior at Barstow, had no idea I sent in a postcard bearing her name. Her card was drawn.

On Thanksgiving evening, my child pushed the lever lighting up my childhood memories.

Christmas display at Sears on the Plaza, circa 1950.

There, like magic, was a breathtaking array of bright, dazzling, twinkling colored lights adorning all the buildings.

Young Kansas ladies shopping for the perfect dress in 1950.

Published on June 6, 1999

Plaza shopping

By Gwen Stephenson-Echard

We always left our shopping trips on the Plaza feeling like queens, albeit exhausted queens.

I lived in Kansas most of my life. It has been less than a year since I moved away, but memories of growing up in the Kansas City area will always be with me.

I was just looking at a picture of my date and me all dressed up for the 1954 homecoming dance at my school, St. Joseph's in Shawnee. That year I was a junior. The photo reminded me of the blue taffeta dress I wore and the shopping trip I bought it on.

Every year on Ascension Thursday, a holy day, the Catholic schools were dismissed. This was the day a group of us girls would make our annual trip to the Country Club Plaza. It was a day to get dressed up, wear makeup, take the bus all the way from Shawnee to the Plaza and shop in some of the most beautiful shops in the city. On the trip there was lots of oohing and ahhing at the beauty and opulence of the houses we passed. We'd also catch up on all the current gossip on this trip.

When we reached the Plaza, we clutched our purses tightly, knowing we had only so much money to spend. My money came from many evenings of baby-sitting — 35 cents an hour in those days. With $30 in my purse, I thought I was rich.

As we walked past the Bristol on our way to a sidewalk cafe, we imagined ourselves to be famous ladies, like Thomas Hart Benton's wife, eating in a very lush restaurant. We walked every inch of the Plaza, obsessing over everything those beautiful windows displayed. I bought the blue taffeta dress and matching shoes at Emery, Bird, Thayer. This was my first trip to the famous department store. In those days, the clerks — and there were many — followed us around, showing us everything and voicing opinions about size, color and design. They were sometimes a pain, but believe me, there are times these days when I wish they were still around. The dress and the shoes would later prove to be a great success with my date and at the dance.

We always left our shopping trips on the Plaza feeling like queens, albeit exhausted queens. We'd get back on the bus and fall asleep on the way home. It wouldn't be long before we were looking forward to next year and another trip to the Plaza.

I'm retired now and living out of state, but I always like to drive through the beautiful Plaza when I'm in town. Even with all the changes, it is still one of the prettiest shopping areas in the country.

Published on November 7, 1999

Plaza Theatre

By Dorothy D. Rowe

The Plaza Theatre in 1929.

My family moved into a house at 47th and Holmes in 1939. We didn't have a car, but we didn't mind. We'd walk to the Plaza and look at the beautiful buildings and fountains. Sometimes we'd go to the Plaza Theatre. And I'd never seen anything like the Nelson art gallery — life-size statues and beautiful paintings.

Then there was the Rockhill Theatre on Troost, with its wonderful organ music to accompany the movies. On Saturday afternoons we'd walk to the library at Paseo High School and bring home books for all of us to read. Mom liked novels with happy endings, Dad read Westerns, my brother liked the Hardy Boys, and I read everything from Nancy Drew to Pearl Buck.

We'd ride the streetcar to other points of interest, such as downtown, where we could shop and have a hot dog at the stand-up counter in Kresge's. I've never found a hot dog that good anywhere else. We'd also go to the Swope Park Zoo and watch the frightening lions, tigers and bears. Sometimes we'd take a picnic lunch. It was a wonderful way for a family to spend an afternoon.

There was also a lot to be said for just staying home. My favorite part of our house was the front porch and the swing. My mother loved to sit in that swing after supper and unwind after her busy day. It was a gathering place for neighbors and friends, too. As I grew older, my boyfriend and I would walk to a movie, maybe stop for a hamburger and then return home to sit on the swing and plan our future.

In those days, streetlights on Holmes were gas lamps. A lamplighter came in the evening to turn up the flame to make a bright light; he'd return in the morning to turn it down. One of these lamps was exactly in front of our porch. The bright light was fine when we had company, but it was too much for a young couple in love. One night my boyfriend climbed the lamppost — they weren't very high — and turned the flame down. It was more romantic that way. He'd do this often, but he always turned the flame back up before he left.

He proposed to me on that porch swing. This house was also where we held our wedding reception, and a few years later when I visited Mom, I sat in the swing with my first baby. My husband and I had three great kids and 57 happy years together. The gas lights and the house are gone now. My dear husband passed away, and I have wonderful memories of a happier time.

We'd walk to the Plaza and look at the beautiful buildings and fountains.

Published on June 14, 1998

Polly's Pop

By Glen Enloe

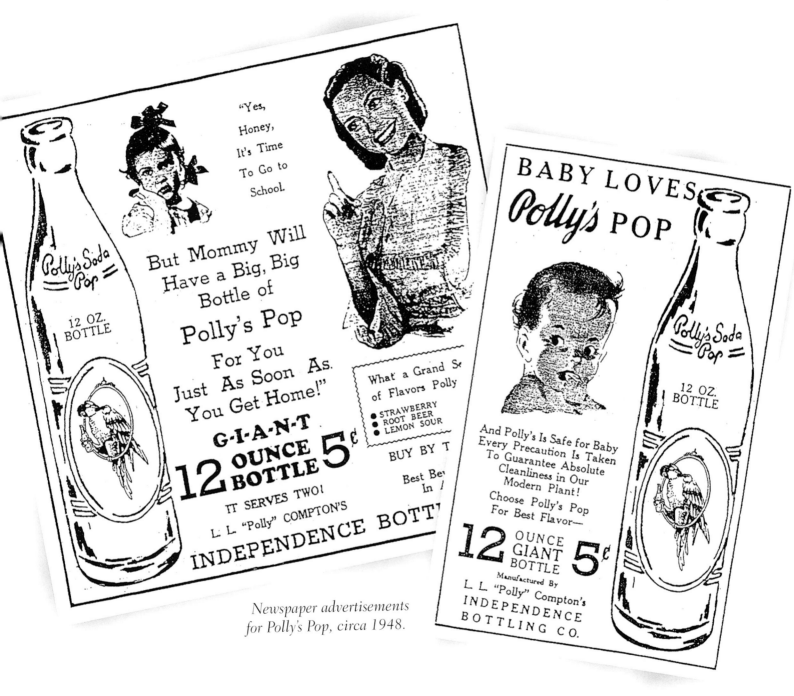

Newspaper advertisements for Polly's Pop, circa 1948.

*S*ummers are a time of dripping, chocolate-shelled ice cream, Popsicles, candy and pop. There was always lots of pop. Not soda, as some Easterners or old-timers called it, but pop. And the best pop of all those summer days was Polly's. Polly's Pop.

In Independence everyone knew about and drank Polly's Pop. Especially Polly's strawberry pop. Could there be anything better in all the world? The dripping, cool sweat from the cold glass bottle oozed down your hand as you slowly tipped it back for that first magnificent gulp of sweet strawberry red perfection.

Yes, Polly's was the hometown pop. My father preferred the tawny brown succulence of Polly's cream soda. But there was actually a wide array of flavors back in those simpler days. There was grape, vanilla, orange, lemon and more. But for some childish reason I stuck with strawberry. There was just nothing better than strawberry then — even my father liked it on those rare occasions when he drank any pop other than cream soda.

And then there were the pop bottles. They accumulated in the garage until my parents issued the ultimatum for me to take them down to the local mom-and-pop store. Somehow the cardboard pop cartons always seemed to disappear, so I had to load up my red wagon with bottles and gently guide it down the sidewalk and across the street for two blocks to Mrs. Chapman's Grocery Store. The biggest problem was getting my wagon full of glass bottles up a flight of concrete steps to the store without breaking half of them. Somehow, I usually managed not to break any, and I would then proudly present my treasure to Mrs. Chapman herself. It seems that back then we only got 2 or 3 cents a bottle for returns. But that was big money, and I would eagerly clutch the new handful of change I got in my sweating palm and hover under the big display case by the door deciding on how to spend the money. Inevitably, I'd buy some button candy and, more than likely, a cold bottle of Polly's strawberry pop. Those were the good old days.

The Polly's Pop factory closed in the late 1950s or early 1960s and was later torn down. Today the site of the old building is a well-kept park that bears the Polly's name. The strawberry and cream pop is long gone. The old empty bottles are sold now as collector's items. Those summers are over. But the sweet taste of hope and another coming summer is still fresh on my lips.

The dripping, cool sweat from the cold glass bottle oozed down your hand as you slowly tipped it back for that first magnificent gulp of sweet strawberry red perfection.

A worker gives a master rod a final polish in 1943 at the wartime Pratt & Whitney Plant at 95th and Troost.

Published on March 18, 2001

Pratt & Whitney engine plant

By Chet Smith

We lived for more than three years with the round-the-clock drone from testing of completed engines.

In the 1940s, during my grade school years, I thought I lived in Kansas City. But actually we lived south of Kansas City. The city limit then was 75th Street, and later 79th.

We lived just south of 92nd Street on Walnut. North of us, an area bounded by 85th and 89th streets and Wornall and Holmes was called Santa Fe Hills. It had newer homes, larger and nicer than houses in my neighborhood. South of 89th Street, our area had a mix of smaller, older homes of various types and was sometimes called "Dogpatch."

I attended Boone grade school at 89th and Wornall for eight years, graduating in 1947. There were no buses, so I walked the half mile to and from school each day with my friends. We walked on narrow oil roads with ditches on each side instead of on sidewalks and curbs. The trek was great in the spring and fall but difficult in the cold and snow of winter. Boone has expanded several times since then, but the original building I attended is still standing and in use today.

During our summer vacations we had big maple trees to climb and could go down to Dykes Branch to fish or swim. That creek is just north of 95th Street and flows into the Blue River.

There was a very small grocery store at 90th and Walnut, but we often walked the seven or eight blocks to 85th Street where the streetcar line had a stop. We would ride the streetcar to Waldo for real shopping, or even downtown to visit the Jones Store or Emery, Bird, Thayer. This southernmost part of the Kansas City public transportation system ran back and forth between Waldo (75th and Wornall) and Dodson (85th and Prospect). It frequently was referred to as the Toonerville Trolley.

During those World War II years I often spent part of each day with my grandparents, as both my stepfather and my mother worked at the Pratt & Whitney engine plant at 95th and Troost. Sometimes they even worked different shifts. This plant made aircraft engines for many of the fighters and bombers used in World War II. We lived for more than three years with the round-the-clock drone from testing of completed engines. That sound became such a part of our lives we didn't even notice until it stopped at the end of the war.

About five years ago I drove through the old neighborhood to reminisce and see what had changed. The familiar scenery brought back a rush of emotions and recollections from the days when I lived south of the border.

Price's Restaurant, at 10th and Walnut, circa early 1950s.

Published on January 14, 2001

Price's lunch counter

By Mabel DeLissa

When Price Candy Co. went out of business last year, closing a plant in Richmond, Mo., it brought back many memories for me. During 1944-45 I frequently had lunch at Price's lunch counter at 10th and Walnut downtown. It was a nice, big place and always busy. I worked at Kansas City Title Insurance Co. on the opposite corner, and Price's was a popular noontime spot for downtown office workers.

The thing I remember about Price's long lunch counter was one of its tasty sandwiches. It was my favorite: whole-wheat bread spread with a generous filling of fluffy Philadelphia cream cheese and sprinkled with black walnuts. Fortified by this crunchy sandwich and a cup of steaming hot coffee, that was all I needed. The cream cheese was a good substitute for meat, a wartime casualty.

One more thing: The sandwich bread at Price's was sliced diagonally, which somehow enhanced the flavor. At home we always sliced sandwiches smack-dab through the middle. It's strange how a simple thing like the way the bread was sliced made that much difference!

If I had a memory book of my experiences during those winter war years, I would have to include the sight of marching WAC members stepping along briskly to their downtown training place; the dreary apartment I shared with another girl from my hometown of Lamar, Mo. (we couldn't get a telephone because of wartime restrictions); and the hushed quiet of the Plaza Theatre after a heavy snowstorm, truly a Christmas card scene as one emerged from the movie house into a sparkling world.

And how could I forget April 12, 1945, when the office came alive after a phone call from one of the wives telling the news of President Roosevelt's death. It was almost quitting time, but no more work was done that day. "Good heavens," I remember thinking. "The new president, Harry Truman, is from my hometown."

It wasn't long before the war was finally over. My roommate went to California to marry her Navy Seabee, and I was offered my old job at the school in Lamar, where I stayed until retirement. I was glad to be back home again. My dad was in failing health, and I was needed there. Besides, I'd had the opportunity of being on my own and making my own decisions. I had proved to myself that I could do it.

Such indelible memories!

Royals: George Brett

By Janet Haskin

George Brett in 1974.

I grew up in the small northeast Kansas town of Onaga (population 750). There wasn't a lot to do for entertainment, so I would always look forward to our family's annual vacation trip to Kansas City.

Each year we stayed at the old Howard Johnson's in Lenexa, where we could enjoy the indoor swimming pool on the hot summer days. Sometimes we would go to Worlds of Fun, too, but our main thrill was getting to go to a Royals baseball game.

George Brett was my favorite player, and I even had to have the same jersey number as him on my softball team back home. I often played third base and batted in the third spot, just like he did. I even tried to be a switch hitter like him, but I couldn't quite master that trick. My dad, who for many years was my coach, sure helped me try, though.

It was a real treat to be able to watch my idol in person — the way he'd slug home runs or make great defensive plays. Of course a trip to Royals Stadium wasn't complete without enjoying some fluffy, pink cotton candy, red and blue snow cones or ice-cold frosty malts that we couldn't get anywhere else.

My dad was an avid Royals fan and told us all about each player on the field. From Amos Otis and Dan Quisenberry to Frank White and Willie Wilson, we knew them all. Even though we made it to only one game a year, we would still watch the Royals on TV or listen to them on the radio back home. The way my dad got worked up when they did something good or bad, you almost felt like you were there in person.

I haven't been to a Royals game for many years, but I still cherish the memories of those wonderful trips to Kansas City with my family. George Brett no longer plays baseball, but I only hope that with the resurgent interest in today's Royals, many kids will be able to enjoy such family outings as I did growing up.

George Brett was my favorite player, and I even had to have the same jersey number as him on my softball team back home.

Santa-Cali-Gon demonstration in 1947.

Published on September 3, 1995

Santa-Cali-Gon

By Laura Howard Downey

Santa-Cali-Gon celebrations were in full swing that balmy evening in 1940 on the square in Independence. I had just won the title of Little Miss Independence and was busy relishing every minute of it, twirling in the gathered skirt of the pink-and-white dress that my mother and Aunty Lilly had made me for the occasion.

The next minute I was being transported into the arms of, what seemed to me, the biggest giant I had ever seen. He was dressed in red, white and blue trousers with a red jacket. He also sported a long white beard and tall blue hat.

"I hear we have the same birthday," he said, "although I think I'm a little older. They say you have lots of kittens. Will you tell me their names?"

I had no intention of giving this troubling stranger any information. And the fact that my parents (who had cautioned me repeatedly never to talk to strangers) seemed to be so pleased was something I couldn't understand.

Then the giant made a strange request. "Will you give me a kiss?" he asked.

Fat chance! I leaned so far out of his arms that he had to catch me to keep me from falling. This seemed to amuse him and he said, "All right, I'll kiss you then," and he did, right on my cheek. With that he good-naturedly returned me to my mother who, surprisingly enough, seemed flustered and embarrassed.

If someone had told me his name then, it wouldn't have meant a thing to me. Much later I learned that the giant was actually a real man campaigning for the office of U.S. senator and was dressed in an Uncle Sam's suit.

His name? Harry S Truman. I was in the arms of greatness and I didn't even know it.

Published on July 9, 2000

Smoking

By Evelyn A. Bartlow

Joan Crawford

Joan Crawford inhaled deeply; Norma Shearer blew smoke rings from a long silver holder; and Garbo "vanted to be alone" with her cigarette.

When I was 14, I wanted to be a glamorous movie star and experience the joy of smoking.

My friend Mary and I decided to walk to the Crown Drug Store at 39th and Woodland and buy one package of Wing cigarettes. We dressed in grown-up-looking clothes — long skirts, white blouses, nylon hose — and slipped on our low Cuban-heel pumps.

We walked from 37th and Wayne to the drugstore. The clerk by the bronze cash register didn't even look up as he rang the 10-cent sale.

We looked around the drugstore and soda fountain to see if any neighbor kids saw us make our covert purchase. No one was there that early Sunday morning.

Mary slid the pack into her large skirt pocket.

We quickly walked the four blocks to her house, kicked off those Cuban pumps and locked the front door. No one was home as her folks were in the Ozarks.

I tore off the cellophane wrapper and divided the cigarettes between us. Ten for Mary and 10 for me. With stick matches from the match-box holder on the kitchen wall, Mary lighted my first cigarette. She watched me suck in smoke and blow it out. I coughed. I lighted her first cig, and she blew smoke in my face.

The room filled with smoke as we continued lighting and puffing on the extras. After each cigarette, we became more lightheaded and our stomachs became queasy. We felt dizzy, nauseated and in need of fresh air. We weren't having fun like Joan, Norma and Greta. But we had paid 10 cents and had to smoke them all to get our money's worth.

To this day neither Mary nor I has smoked another cigarette.

When I was 14, I wanted to be a glamorous movie star and experience the joy of smoking.

Torey Southwick and Ol' Gus.

Published on December 19, 1999

Southwick on TV

By Vicki McCanse Jones

"Vicki, what am I thankful for and why?" my 8-year-old sister Betsy asked idly one late October day. The television blared afternoon children's shows in the background. Barely glancing up from my book, I muttered, "Love, because it is warm and friendly." Evidently I had been reading Charles Schulz's book "Happiness Is a Warm Puppy," but plagiarism means little to a 9-year-old. Betsy slowly recorded my words with a fat pencil and finished coloring a turkey the size of her hand on the postcard, which my father mailed the next day.

A month later we were excitedly getting ready for an incredible outing. Betsy had been chosen as a finalist on the Torey Southwick TV show. Mom ironed and starched our best flocked dresses and shined our patent leather shoes. I was to escort my younger sister on the city bus to where Dad would meet us downtown. Mom walked us down the icy hill in the snow and waited with us at the Morningside and Brookside stop. She waved as we hopped eagerly onto the 63rd and Brookside bus, and reminded us once more of the number of our destination.

Soon we saw Dad at 11th and Main, across from Macy's. We pulled the silver wire and ran down the steep metal steps to hug him. He walked us to the television studio in time for the filming. The room was packed with noisy children, but only five would be named winners of the annual "I Am Thankful For" contest. I watched with intense curiosity as Torey Southwick announced the winners for 1960. Suddenly Betsy's name was read and before my very eyes she walked over to a mountain of toys and selected a Chatty Cathy doll as her prize. We had been ogling this very toy in the dime store for months, only daring to dream about receiving such an expensive and coveted toy for Christmas. The doll would actually talk when her ring was pulled! And now my little sister, with her bright-red pigtails bobbing in delight, was clutching a brand-new Chatty Cathy.

"Betsy," Torey said, "you wrote such a sweet postcard about why you were thankful for love ..." To my horror I heard the words I had suggested being read on live TV: "... because it is warm and friendly."

"But I wrote that!" I wailed in disbelief. The television audience must have heard. The host surely did, because he hurriedly said, "And the drawing of the turkey was wonderful, too!"

Later, as reconciliation, he told Betsy to share the Chatty Cathy with me. He obviously did not have two daughters so close in age waiting at home for him. Still, I learned a valuable lesson about taking credit for one's own ideas.

141

Published on June 25, 2000

Starlight: beginnings

By Martha Nance

Starlight Theatre, official opening, in 1951.

The year 1950 was a momentous one for me and Kansas City.

I graduated from high school that year and took a train to Kansas City to work to earn college money for the following fall. My sister, who had come down the year before, knew the ropes and guided me from Union Station to the house where we rented a room from a neat lady named Mary Lou. We lived on 40th Street Way, just off Main Street. Mary Lou taught us to play canasta; I got a job typing at Beta Sigma Phi over on Broadway; and I bought myself a pair of high-heeled red shoes to wear to work. At last, I was a grown-up!

Everyone was excited about the celebrations for the city's centennial year. A grand pageant was to be presented in the new Starlight Theatre, which was to be finished the following year. A temporary theater would be in place for the pageant that summer, and the show was scheduled to run four weeks.

When the call went out for volunteers to be in the pageant, my sister and I signed up. We were assigned to be extras during the fourth week of the show's run. We were told when and where to move around on stage and were given costumes to wear. I think we may have had one run-through actually on the Starlight stage. In those days we could easily reach the new theater by using the wonderful trolley buses that ran all over the city.

The pageant turned out to be a huge success, and when our turn to perform finally arrived, a fifth week of performances was added. So we went every night for two weeks to put on our costumes and march around the stage in the spotlights at the proper time. I believe I was dressed as a Miss Liberty when I came on stage during the grand finale. It was all very exciting, and the audience loved it and cheered loudly at the end. We had a great time. I never did see the pageant from the front, but I'm sure it was about Kansas City's history and growth into a great city.

Just as the last performance on the last day ended, it began to rain, so my sister and I — still dressed in our costumes — raced for the bus stop. As we arrived there, completely drenched, a car pulled up, and a man called out, "Would you girls like a ride?" Having come from a small town where everyone did that sort of thing, we happily accepted. The driver asked where we wanted to go and seemed quite disappointed when he realized how young we were and that we really did just want a ride to 40th and Main. But he let us off where we had requested and wished us luck.

I still have the commemorative medal they gave me as a souvenir of my "debut" on stage. And today I enjoy sitting in Starlight to watch the performance from the audience. But I don't accept rides from strange men!

I believe I was dressed as a Miss Liberty when I came on stage during the grand finale.

Ethel Merman, circa 1953.

Published on August 22, 1999

Starlight: Ethel Merman

By Mary Carolyn Wilson

Full house at Starlight Theatre in 1951.

Many feelings have changed since the early 1950s in regard to Swope Park and Starlight Theatre, except for one very important feeling: a little grade-school girl's wide-eyed dreams of one day being center stage in musical theater. Let me take you back to 1952 in Kansas City.

Ethel Merman, the great musical-comedy star, was coming to our town to star in "Call Me Madam." I was 12 at the time and planning, in six years, to move to New York City to break into musical theater.

I begged my mother to let me go stand in line at Starlight in the July heat (that part hasn't changed) to be one of the first 100 people to obtain free tickets for the back row. Who cared if the seats were in the back row? Ms. Merman had the great loud alto voice to sing without needing a microphone! However, the sound system was well in

place that night.

Well, I got the free tickets for my mother and myself, and I was beside myself with feelings of joy and anticipation. Now, what to wear? I had heard that people who attended the outdoor theater dressed in their finest clothes. So I had my hair done at the old Starlight Beauty Shop on Swope Parkway, and I put on my nylon blouse with daisies at the neckline, embossed skirt and white gloves. I was all set to go.

Finally, as my mother and I took our seats in the back row, the lights dimmed, a spotlight came on and out walked this incredible show woman. I lip-synced right along with Ethel because, of course, I knew the "Call Me Madam" score, having bought it at Luyben's Music Store on Main Street. I'd performed those same songs at the Music Hall with the Virginia Loncar Kiddies on Parade dance academy.

I didn't end up going to New York City; I chose marriage and children. But all these years later, there's a 5-year-old girl tugging at my sleeve saying, "Grandma (the sweetest word in the English language), please, please take me to see 'Annie' at Starlight tonight!" This is my granddaughter, Lydia. Never mind that it is 95 degrees outside. Lydia knows the complete score from "Annie." Guess who taught her the music?

As my granddaughter begs me to take her to Starlight, I'm reminded of another grade-school daydreamer who may have had the voice, dancing ability and showmanship to become a great musical comedy star but lacked one main ingredient: drive and ambition. But everyone deserves a second chance, and I'll get that chance in 12 years. I'm planning to move to New York, and I'm taking someone with me who has enough drive for 10 Ethel Mermans. I'm taking Lydia.

Published on August 20, 1995

Starlight: working there

By Susan Kelly Powers

*Jack Jones as Curley, and Linda Michele as Laurey, in the
1966 Starlight Theatre production of "Oklahoma!"*

*D*uring the summer of 1966 at Starlight, rain dampened just one performance. Striking airplanes were silent. And I left the rehearsal pavilion with hands swollen from clapping and clasping all afternoon, in a song called "Hello, Hello There."

We were the resident choral ensemble, and for 12 weeks the Starlight backstage became our world. It was like being sealed into Biosphere 2. Our mission: sing and dance our way though eight shows for 70 nights running. Our reward: union pay and an Actor's Equity card.

We rehearsed by day and performed by night. Our standing date Saturday night after performing was to rehearse Monday's new show, sometimes until 2 a.m. The sun was painfully bright the next morning after that double dose of spotlights.

People on the outside thought our life was glamorous. My audition was on TV. A journalist captured me in color. Then a young singer friend visited in awe.

But the difference between her perception and reality was as wide as the Starlight stage. For every beautiful scene under lights, there was blood, sweat and grime by heat of day. We sang, danced and marched for three drill sergeants cleverly disguised as a chorus master obsessed with diction, an ensemble director programmed for marching and a choreographer bent on perfection. The grime came from Texas Dirt makeup, used for painting our skin during two weeks each of "Flower Drum Song" and "The King and I." It seemed impossible to remove.

Throughout the summer, stars like Kansas City's Dorothy Coulter ("Desert Song"), Jack Jones and Linda Michele ("Oklahoma!") mixed and mingled with us. Gisele MacKenzie ("The King and I"), Betty White and Allen Ludden ("Bells are Ringing") included us in parties. Gary Lewis ("Bye Bye Birdie") and Don Ameche ("How to Succeed in Business without Really Trying") came and went.

After "Guys and Dolls," there was only one show left. No more daytime rehearsals. I reentered the outside world in short excursions, shuttling Downtown to shop, visiting a museum with my cousin and going out to lunch with a friend.

It was great to be back. I had learned a lot. Life in a pressure capsule wasn't for me. But that experience would open doors for me as I pursued other aspects of my music career after college.

When the applause finally died away, I debriefed at a distant lake where I was cleansed forever of Texas Dirt.

For 12 weeks the Starlight backstage became our world.

Dorothy Coulter in 1966.

Published on October 27, 1996

Strawberry Hill

By George Kvaternik

Baseball on Strawberry Hill, in 1957.

We stayed close to our Strawberry Hill neighborhood when I was growing up in the late 1920s.

We didn't pay much attention to the homes. They were pretty much alike: 25-foot lot, front porch, brick walk around the side leading to a grape arbor and garden, a shed, an outhouse. Nor did we notice the neatness, though most of us spent Saturday mornings helping to clean up the inside and outside of these houses in Kansas City, Kan.

Playing was our real world. We made scooters by fastening half a skate to the front of a 2-by-4 board and the other half to the back. Then we nailed a crate on front, with a piece of wood across that for handle bars. Marbles were a must, with a local boy winning the city championship.

The main paved hill was a safe play area because there were few cars. We played hockey with a small can and broomsticks. Our slingshots kept away any bad dogs. We played "run, sheep, run" in the evenings and snatched pieces of ice from the iceman's truck — a daring trick — though he seemed to watch and grin.

We sailed coffee can lids off the bluff top. And a half-mile-long dump, with its adjacent railroad tracks and Kaw River, made for good exploring. Between a couple of the tracks, a spring formed three small ponds. One was perfect for swimming in the summer. We caught crawdads in another and cooked a tasty after-swim treat in tin cans. For a nickel we could go see a movie, serial, comedy, cartoon and the news. For a dime we

could ride around the alleys on one of the huge draft horses from the vinegar works.

We earned our money helping unload grapes at night for people who made wine. (We weren't above stashing a bunch or two in the bushes to retrieve later.) Neighbor families also brought cabbage by the truckload and made sauerkraut. Women cut up the cabbage, and the heaviest boy in the family got to stomp it down in barrels — after being given one heck of an inspection for clean feet.

When the Great Depression gripped the nation, we kids were only vaguely aware of it. What we were aware of was that our neighborhood was a wonderful place, where people lived in harmony.

A game of marbles in progress, circa 1945.

Playing was our real world.

A streetcar southbound on the Country Club Line, in 1956.

Published on May 29, 1994

Streetcars: riding to school

By Esther M. Gloe

School buses were almost unheard of when I was a girl, and most public transportation was by streetcar.

Each afternoon when I see my middle-school neighbor get off the big yellow school bus in front of the driveway, I am reminded of the Dinkey, the streetcar we once rode to Westport Junior High School.

School buses were almost unheard of when I was a girl, and most public transportation was by streetcar. The Dinkey ran up and down 39th Street, from Main Street to State Line Road. At the west end of the line was Bell Memorial Hospital (now the University of KansasMedical Center). At the east end were Westport Junior and Senior high schools.

The Dinkey got its nickname because it was only half as big as the other streetcars. At the end of the line the Dinkey's driver always had to get out, disconnect the trolley pole from the cable above, pull it all the way around the car and reconnect it to the cable at the other end. Then the Dinkey could head back the other way. Often the school boys aboard would run around to help the driver at the end of the line. Cars on the street waited patiently for the transfer.

The Dinkey always had great drivers, very understanding. I remember one rainy afternoon in particular. I got on the Dinkey fearfully because I had run out of nickels. All I had were a few five-cent tokens from the school cafeteria. I asked the driver whether I could sell him one and buy it back on Monday. He grinned.

"You kids sure do run out of nickels on Friday. I'll take your token and put a nickel in for you. I take these tokens up to the Westport Junior office every week or so and sell them back to the cashier."

I almost cried when I said, "Oh, thank you so much."

Some of the boys who rode the Dinkey were daring. They would sit in the very back seats and dangle their legs out the windows. They'd even try to kick the other Dinkey as it went the other way on its track. The drivers never protested; I guess they knew nobody's legs could be that long.

By the time spring came, we girls had figured out that by walking home we could save our nickels and spend them on ice cream cones. My mother was very surprised the first time she saw me walking down 39th Street with an ice-cream cone in my hand instead of riding the Dinkey, but she didn't forbid my fun.

Even today, only one two-block walk to school sticks in my mind. That morning the paper boy stood on the corner of 39th and Main streets crying his headline: "Hitler wants peace! A piece here and a piece there!" Changes were on the way.

151

Stepping aboard the No. 50 Troost streetcar, circa 1940.

Published on January 11, 1998

Streetcars: riding to work

By Marjorie Eitel

Inside a streetcar, circa 1940.

To me, memories of the streetcar are interwoven with my years of working in the city.

Years ago when I had a job in downtown Kansas City and lived in a trailer park on State Avenue in Kansas City, Kan., I used to ride the streetcar to work. I worked in the billing department for a wholesale jewelry company, Jules Borel and Sons.

I would catch the streetcar on Minnesota Avenue and ride across the river bridge all the way to Eleventh and Walnut. It was hard to tell which made more clatter — the old manual billing machine I ran or the streetcar. But I soon got used to the ride — the regular clackety-clack of the wheels on the track, the "ding, ding" of the bell, squealing brakes and all — and would sit back to enjoy the trip and watch people.

My sister-in-law rode to work, too. Sometimes we managed to catch the same car, but we were lucky if we got to sit together. It was too noisy to carry on a conversation most of the time anyway.

In those days, lots of people rode the streetcars. I could usually get a seat in the morning, but on the way home it would be so crowded, I sometimes had to stand up, holding onto a strap all the way. It was quite a trick to keep my balance with all the stops and starts and the swaying. One evening a fight broke out over a seat, and I got off several blocks before my stop so I wouldn't get involved. Another time we hit a car, and police came aboard to question passengers.

Usually there was not much excitement, just a long bumpy ride. In summer the windows were lowered and the breeze felt good, especially when we crossed the bridge and got a whiff of the Missouri River. In winter the ride was cold.

To me, memories of the streetcar are interwoven with my years of working in the city. I remember meeting my sister-in-law for lunch and shopping. We would eat stuffed peppers at Myron Green's Cafeteria. She liked to shop at Jones' bargain basement. I liked to visit the two big five-and-dime stores that were side by side: Kresge and Woolworth. I had to be careful not to buy more than I could handle in case I had to stand and hang onto a strap on the ride home.

Christmas in the city was especially beautiful to a girl from the country. I remember one year Emery, Bird, Thayer had a window display of an animated Mr. and Mrs. Santa Claus and lots of elves. The scene even had sound effects — including the "Ho, ho, ho" of Santa's laughter.

I have to say that anyone who never rode a streetcar and never worked downtown in those days missed an interesting adventure.

Published on February 27, 2000

Streetcars: a thrilling ride

By Mary Lou Roberts

The Ninth Street Incline in 1904; the Eighth Street Tunnel is seen in the background to the left.

Remember when a nickel bought you a ride across the city and the state line? You could hop onto the Dinkey bus at 12th and Belmont, transfer to the streetcar at 12th and Jackson and then travel across the Kansas-Missouri state line, ending the trip at 18th and Kansas Avenue in Kansas City, Kan. The streetcar tracks were on the north side of the 23rd Street Viaduct just west of the American Royal Building and had absolutely no rail over the Kansas River.

What an exciting ride! If you sat on the right side, you could look out the open window of the streetcar as it made the critical turn before crossing the river. A chill of pending disaster always accompanied me on that ride: What if we didn't navigate the turn? Would the streetcar be hurled into the depths of the river? Of course, that never happened, but admittedly the ride fueled a child's vivid imagination. The sights and sounds of the city, and oh, the smells. The windows were open during good weather, and each section of the city emitted its own distinctive aroma. Downtown always smelled much like burnt toast and was at once dismissed as we approached the stockyards. Now that was an aroma you could not disregard.

By the time I reached junior high, we had what we called "streetcar parties." Our parents would rent a streetcar, much as you would today rent a limousine. We junior high groups would board the streetcar at 18th and Kansas Avenue and would "party" (with sing-alongs and games) the entire trip to Swope Park, where parents would be waiting with refreshments. The streetcar then made the return trip with the partying teen group back to our original site of departure, through a bustling cityscape and that wonderful tunnel on the west bluff above the West Bottoms.

On rare occasions when my folks could afford the 35 cents, I was allowed to take the Trailways bus from the downtown terminal to visit my aunt, uncle and cousins who lived in Lenexa. This much-planned-for trip took at least an hour and a half but was well worth the price. It was like a visit to a far-off land, with beautiful pastures embracing contented cattle grazing on the sweet-smelling prairie grasses.

There simply weren't many local destinations that you could not reach back then for a nickel. Our modes of transportation were not necessarily rapid, but they were dependable. For a nickel, you could escape to new worlds, new surroundings and wondrous new experiences. In retrospect, one other important factor becomes prominent: My nickel travels as a child were safe.

Times have changed. Without the automobile, our children would be severely confined to their respective neighborhoods. And sadly, they will never experience the clang of the trolley car or know the thrill of exploration the trolleys afforded us in that long-ago, tranquil era.

What if we didn't navigate the turn? Would the streetcar be hurled into the depths of the river?

Published on April 25, 1999

Summe Dairy

By Mary Detrich

Employees of the Summe Dairy, circa 1928.

Young people today probably don't realize that years ago milk and bread deliveries were made to homes by horse and wagon. After graduating from Northeast High School in 1928, my future husband, Fred Detrich, went to work for Summe Dairy, serving a milk route with a horse and wagon. He was the shortest driver and had the largest horse, a Clydesdale named Dutch.

The dairy was at 27th and Jackson then. Fred's route covered the area of Jackson to Benton, 15th to 27th Street. The men worked from 1:30 a.m. till after noon. The salary was $16 a week; drivers got two days off a month. After their deliveries, the drivers had to go back over part of their route each day to collect what people owed. If a customer didn't pay or had moved without paying, the money came out of the driver's salary. When Fred was through with the route, he could rest in the back of the wagon and Dutch would take them back to the dairy. The wagon would come within inches of parked cars but never hit one, and Dutch always stopped at red lights.

The first day on the route, coming to the bridge on Agnes over the terminal tracks, Dutch ran across at full speed. Fred asked the barn manager if he knew why. It turned out that one time Dutch was on the bridge when a train going under blew its whistle — which scared him so badly that he always ran full tilt across from then on.

On the route there was an entire block of apartments, back to back. Fred could take his carriers of milk and serve the buildings on one street, then the other, and Dutch would go around the block and meet him. You can't get a truck to do that!

One icy morning, going south of 15th on Jackson, Dutch found he could get traction by putting his big hooves on the granite cobblestones on each side of the streetcar tracks. Before long, several streetcars were lined up behind the wagon. A motorman got off his streetcar, thinking he could get the horse to move from the tracks. But when he grabbed the reins, Dutch reared up and pawed the air with hooves as big as dinner plates. Dutch would have hit him if the motorman hadn't decided to get back on the streetcar and slowly follow the horse and wagon to the dairy.

There was a pear tree on the route. Dutch knew when the fruit was ripe and refused to go past the tree unless he could have a pear. But he never wanted them when he knew they were past their prime.

In the late 1930s, the dairy moved to a new building on the southeast corner of 15th and Benton, and by that time trucks were beginning to be used for delivery. Finally, Dutch was retired to the country. The dairy building was torn down when Interstate 70 was built.

He was the shortest driver and had the largest horse, a Clydesdale named Dutch.

Swope Park in 1929.

Published on July 2, 2000

Swope Park: sleeping there

By Lloyd Hellman

We would load the car with the food and a card table and head for Swope Park.

"Let's go up on the hill," my father would say nearly every night during the summers of the 1930s. He was referring to Swope Park, that marvelous expanse of green grass at Meyer Boulevard and Swope Parkway. This was before air conditioning in homes. The Newman Theatre alone at 12th and Main streets had refrigerated air, and the rest of the city sweltered before oscillating fans that passed the hot wet air from one space to another, providing little relief.

The year 1936 was a record breaker for high summer heat and low economic times. But my dad had a car to haul his ladders and tools, and my mom would pack up supper, including casseroles carried in slings made from dishtowels. We would load the car with the food and a card table and head for Swope Park.

They told me I was a beneficiary of Swope Park's cooling breezes when I was less than a week old, having been born in June 1930. I know one of my first memories includes lying on a blanket looking up at the stars (millions more than can be seen now because of light and haze near the city). I would pretend to break one of the brighter ones open, and bicycles and wagons and shiny toys of every child's desire would pour forth; I would describe them to my cousin or friend lying on the blanket with me.

My dad played pitch, a stripped-down sort of bridge game, under the streetlight near the concession stand, which was adjacent to the band shell. My mom preferred the higher ground across the road from the concession stand where the best breezes blew. (This plot of ground later became known among its frequenters as "Little Jerusalem" because the poorer Jews of the city swelled its population to as many as 200 on a good night.) The children would swing high on the swings until the chains buckled, and the pre-teens learned a little more about life than was taught at school.

Colonel Swope gave a place of pastoral relief to the residents of our city. These new Americans and their native-born children complemented his gift by making it a place of community gathering as well as a respite from the summer heat.

Aerial view of Swope Swimming Pool, circa 1945.

Swope Park: swimming pools

By Sondra Dee Cooper

Published on July 18, 1999

There we could watch the divers swim underwater through glass windows below the diving pool, and of course we'd swim, too, in the enormous center pool.

It was a cool summer morning in Kansas City, and I'd been getting ready for my swimming lesson at Paseo High School. Mother had enrolled me in the beginners swimming class sponsored by the Kansas City park department and the Kansas City School District. I would take 5 or 10 cents with me for a stop at the penny candy store on the way home.

Then I'd casually walk along dreaming of going swimming at the Swope Park Pool. There we could watch the divers swim underwater through glass windows below the diving pool, and of course we'd swim, too, in the enormous center pool.

Yesterday had been a wonderful family day. We'd met our cousins for a barbecue at Swope Park. Our ankles had been carefully covered with powdered sulfur to repel the chiggers. We'd found the best picnicking area. While our moms began setting the table, my sister, cousin and I were off swinging on the swings. Our fathers left to go get firewood somewhere near the park entrance.

Summer back then, 50-plus years ago, unofficially began when the canvas-awning truck made its rounds putting up awnings everywhere. Mother would brew iced tea and put away our winter clothes. We'd play hide-and-go-seek and chase lightning bugs. We'd also go exploring — in the woods for arrowheads and in creeks for crawdads and minnows.

Who could forget the beautiful rose garden or the band concerts or the wonderful natural stone-stepped water fountains at Loose Park? We made clover chains and hollyhock dolls that summer and delighted in the cool velvet bluegrass under our feet.

I'm back living in Kansas City now after 31 years away. I never thought I'd miss the tall, shady trees and creeks here as much as I did. Soon three of my grandchildren will visit. They're enrolled in swimming lessons. I hope to fill their two weeks with memories of a Kansas City summer.

Published on January 2, 2000

Tarzan

By Ann Cain Tibbets

Glenn Morris as Tarzan in 1938.

These days it sometimes seems that every young person is attached to an electronic device of some type, happily hitting keys, listening to bells or whistles go off and often oblivious to anyone around. Watching them, I can't help but wonder how they would have entertained themselves during the Depression. Even if computer games had existed, few would have had the money to buy them.

Those years called for both penny-pinching and creativity for the active kids that we were. In the large, flat back yard of one of the neighborhood houses, we played croquet with a vengeance, boys and girls alike. The sound of wooden mallets hitting wooden balls to accompanying cheers or groans is one of the staples of our memory banks.

And there were the yard games: Tap the Icebox, Red Rover, King of the Mountain, I Spy, tag. We played until dusk sent our mothers to various doors to summon us home.

Sometimes we picked the white clover in our yards, knotted the end of the stem around the head of another clover and repeated this until we had a rather impressive rope of flowers. This we'd stretch across the street, waiting gleefully for a car to lumber by and break the chain. That really was a great moment when our white rope departed, festooning the bumper of the passing car.

Some of the younger boys in the neighborhood worshipped at the shrine of Tarzan, King of the Apes. The kids were about 6 and ran from tree to tree, attempting the Tarzan yell as they went. One of the mothers found some material somewhere, and the moms produced the most startling Tarzan costumes ever seen. These unlikely "leopard skin" outfits — blaring yellow with circles of red and blue all over — were the most sensational successes of the summer. No self-respecting leopard would have claimed them, but the small Tarzans adored their costumes.

The girls often played with paper dolls, some cut from the fashion pages of a newspaper, others drawn by what I now know was an incredibly talented young girl in the neighborhood. We would give her lists of the outfits we wanted for our dolls, and she would create them in watercolor with lines and shading that went far beyond things drawn by other kids her age.

One more affordable form of entertainment was found at 55th and Brookside Boulevard. Along the side of what's now an antiques shop and tearoom, there was a wooden sidewalk that led to the rear of the building. A tiny shop there offered jigsaw puzzles to rent. For about a quarter, my mother would rent a gigantic puzzle and put it on a card table, and we kids would spend hours completing it. To this day I have not found another place that rented jigsaw puzzles, but the lady who thought of it earned her living that way.

So we played and had fun, and here I sit writing all about it on a computer. I wouldn't go back even if I could, but it was a great time.

Some of the younger boys in the neighborhood worshipped at the shrine of Tarzan, King of the Apes.

Shirley Temple

Published on December 10, 1995

Temple's curls

By Margaret Montgomery

*I told the beauty operator
that I wanted to look just
like Shirley Temple.*

In the 1940s, farm children didn't get to the movies very often. I was in the sixth grade before I saw my first Shirley Temple movie. Never again would I be satisfied with my straight, stringy hair.

"Mother, I just have to have curls like Shirley Temple!" I said as I burst into the kitchen where my mother was working.

"But you don't. Your hair is straight and fine," my mother informed me.

"I could get a permanent!"

"A permanent might ruin your hair, and besides, they're expensive. I don't know where you'd get the money."

"I'll earn it. How could I ruin this hair?" I wailed. "Please, Mother. I just have to get a permanent. I want to look just like she did in the movies."

Walking by the beauty shop, I had seen those women with electric wires hanging from a thing that looked like a chandelier. They

didn't seem to be in pain, but I felt queasy as I thought about it. I put my fears aside.

The next week, I baked a cake for the church social, and one of the ladies was so impressed that she asked if I would bake one for her. She paid me a dollar, which was exactly what I needed for my permanent.

The following Saturday my mother escorted me to the beauty shop and left me. Shyly, I told the beauty operator that I wanted to look just like Shirley Temple. She started putting things in my hair and my head began to wobble from the weight.

"There now, we have you all rolled," she said as she scooted me under the chandelier machine and started hooking the wires to each curl. I was shaking like a leaf.

"It doesn't hurt one bit," she assured me.

After what seemed liked hours,

she came back.

"You've got curls," she said. "Now, I'll just set it, dry it, and you'll be all done."

She put my head under another gadget that was like a giant bonnet. I was sure I'd burn to a crisp before the operator came to my rescue.

"You're dry," she said. "I'll just take down these curlers and comb you out nice and pretty."

I looked in the mirror. I couldn't believe it! "Is that really me?"

"Yep. That's you, honey. How do you like it?"

"I love it," I whispered.

I kept my Shirley Temple image until my mother insisted I wash my hair. It didn't much matter that from the first wash job my beautiful hairdo turned into an uncontrollable fuzz. One of my dreams had come true. I did look like Shirley Temple, if only for a week!

165

Published on November 15, 1998

Thanksgiving turkeys

By Eugene J. Ashley

About a week before Thanksgiving, the eighth-grade male students at my grade school in Kansas City, Kan., would visit all the parish members to collect funds to buy two live turkeys.

On the day before the holiday, during the 90-minute lunchtime, the two nun teachers would stay the entire time in their living quarters above the school.

During this time the teacher's desk would be cleared off, then piled high with food — mainly canned goods from all the children coming back from lunch at their homes.

Meanwhile the two oldest male students, with the money collected, would purchase two live turkeys at Mathe's meat market on Central Avenue.

At 1 p.m., the nuns would enter the decorated classroom and would be greeted by two live turkeys running around the room, along with a lot of excited children. The nuns always acted surprised at this annual event.

No schoolwork was done the remainder of the day — only games and recess. During this time those two oldest boys would take the two live turkeys back to Mathe's to kill and dress. One turkey would be given to the pastor and the other to the nuns that evening.

St. Casimeir's was a Lithuanian Catholic grade school, in existence from 1923 until 1947. It was one block off Eighth Street and Central Avenue in Kansas City, Kan. It was converted to apartments and is still standing.

Illustration by Lisa Morgan

The nuns would enter the decorated classroom and would be greeted by two live turkeys running around the room, along with a lot of excited children.

Tower Theatre

By M.J. Wade

Harry Blackstone Sr. the Magician in 1949.

In 1935, when I was growing up in the Northeast area of Kansas City, I had a magical experience at the Tower Theatre downtown. In those days the Tower offered live vaudeville acts between screenings of the day's major film presentation. For my eighth birthday my Aunt Sis treated me to a Saturday matinee performance of the world-famous Blackstone the Magician. Little did I know that it would prove to be one of the most embarrassing events of my childhood.

As fate would have it, I was beckoned to the stage during the show along with several other youngsters. We were to assist the great Blackstone as he caused a tiny white bird, bamboo cage and all, to disappear.

In the harsh glare of the stage lights, the magician cupped his hands around the caged bird and asked us children to place our hands over his. He then commanded us to look into his eyes and let nothing break our concentration. After we were all in place Blackstone opened his eyes wide and stared out over the audience. He began to chant a series of deep-throated, sing-song incantations and started swaying from side to side.

Mesmerized by the chanting and weaving, we began to sway along with him. Then, without warning, Blackstone gave forth with an ear-splitting yell. As we children jumped with fright, the bird and the cage miraculously shot up into the sleeve of the magician's shiny black coat. There was, however, a problem.

As the little cage collapsed before its trip up the illusionist's sleeve, it ensnared my little finger, causing my hand and wrist to vanish along with the tiny bird. The audience began to laugh. My knees literally shook as I stood there certain that I was going to incur the wrath of the tall, silver-haired man who loomed over me.

However, to my surprise, he smiled at me. He then reached down and gently shook my elbow, thus freeing my finger from the cage. After I slowly withdrew my hand from his sleeve, he bowed graciously in my direction.

I was mortified with embarrassment as I ran from the stage along with the other kids. Aunt Sis later explained that a long elastic band concealed in Blackstone's coat had provided the necessary force to snap the caged bird up into the sleeve.

As we rode the Northeast line streetcar home, I vowed that whatever magic may have been employed that day, I would never again volunteer to be a magician's helper.

Tower Theatre, circa 1945.

We were to assist the great Blackstone as he caused a tiny white bird, bamboo cage and all, to disappear.

Toy boats: Lake Verona Park

By Michael Graff

Boys with sailboats at the mirror pool at 62nd and Ward Parkway.

I saluted and the ship was launched.

Grandpa took me to Lake Verona Park every Sunday. There, of course, were swings, and a slide and a seesaw and monkey bars and water fountains.

And there was a large goldfish pond, where little boys in striped T-shirts and short pants (like me) sailed their toy boats.

My boat was named the H.M.S. Victory II, after the H.M.S. Victory, the flagship of Admiral Horatio Nelson, decimator of the combined Napoleonic fleets in the Battle of Trafalgar, 1805. With blazing cannons, the admiral won glory, fame and immortality. He lost something much greater, however — his life.

The Victory II was "scratchbuilt" by me and Grandpa. The keel was a fruit crate sawed to the shape of a ship's hull. Dowels for the masts and yard arms. Pillow ticking for sails. Kite string for rigging and upholstery tacks for gunports.

Sunday came at last. Grandpa watched as I took my place among my peers pondside. The Victory II was almost ready to sail. All that was missing was the crew. I conscripted a Popsicle stick covered with ants, and one by one they filed aboard. A plump June bug portrayed Admiral Nelson.

I saluted and the ship was launched. Now the Victory II was able to hold its own, and one boy became especially jealous. He became even more so when a slight infraction of the "law of the pond" occurred — our boats collided. The boy picked up a rock and hurled it at the Victory II.

The shock of the blow sent the Victory II down, and the entire crew — or so I thought — was washed overboard. My eyes filled with tears. The boy laughed, collected his schooner and disappeared into villainous history.

Grandpa dried my tears, bought me some ice cream and took the tangled hulk back to the car. Amazingly, five of the crew survived! So, on the way home, Grandpa stopped at the hobby shop and bought, yes, an ant farm.

My guess about Admiral Nelson not surviving was right. There was a little green smudge on a ripped sail of the fallen mast. Anyway, we had the land lovers who would never again have to answer to the call of the sea, er, pond. And they lived happily ever after.

Examining a French textile at the Nelson-Atkins Art Museum, in 1953.

Published on February 25, 2001

Trip to town: with family

By Justyn Lair Graham

Kansas City was a different world from the farm in northwest Missouri where I grew up.

The Burlington Zephyr streamlined train was new — tops in rail transportation in 1934. We rode in luxury: Fresh flowers adorned our table in the dining car, where Mom and I had hot chocolate.

The cavernous train station at Kansas City was a Taj Mahal to a 7-year-old boy. But the fun had just begun.

Everywhere there were wonders to behold: the war memorial with its smoking column, buildings taller than trees, one-car electric trains that ran on tracks in the middle of the street — to name only a few. Kansas City was a different world from the farm in northwest Missouri where I grew up.

A Yellow Cab took us to the home of relatives on Chestnut Street. The next day, Saturday, was a workday for them. My aunt was a saleslady at Grant's on Main Street. My imagination did not exceed the number of wondrous things to buy. The nearby Kresge and Woolworth dime stores were wonderlands of variety. An ingenious machine provided both entertainment and delicious treats as automatic spatulas turned swimming doughnuts at just the right time to produce an irresistible product. The sparkling-clean lunch counters appeased appetites at any time of day. The stores had clothes, lamps, books and toys, toys, toys — a magnetic attraction for this kid. I still have the Pan American China Clipper airplane and the iron Chrysler Airflow toy car. They both have many miles on them by now.

Mom bought a beautiful coat at Peck's. An industrious revolving staircase with moving wooden "steps" transported one effortlessly (but not noiselessly) to a second floor, where a talented pianist in the music department would play your selections of sheet music and make you wish you could play that well.

And at night, the city did not sleep, at least not at Fairyland Park. I threw darts, tossed hoops and became airborne on the giant slide. I rode the merry-go-round so many times that the operator gave me a free ride.

I was ready to visit the animals at the zoo before sunrise. I gave the bears a lunch of peanuts. The snakes were scary, the lions roared and the monkeys put on a show just for me.

Was I ready to rest? No way! There were tall buildings to explore, hamburgers to be eaten and air-conditioned theaters to visit. But Mom was not about to let other cultural opportunities of this metropolitan adventure go untapped. The museum and art gallery were next on the list.

The dream trip of my young life was over all too soon. We boarded a Jefferson Lines bus at the Pickwick Hotel station for the ride home.

My life had changed. I had been to Kansas City!

Published on September 28, 1997

Trip to town: with school

By Ruth Smethers

Rooftop view of the Stockyards' livestock pens and stock runways, circa 1945.

When I graduated from Eugene Field School in Manhattan, Kan., in 1941, the most important event of the year was the sixth-grade trip to Kansas City. It was our reward for completing grade school.

Every detail of that trip was planned down to the last minute. We were on a schedule tighter than a fire drill. We had our seat mates and partners, we had to stay with our group and not wander off, and be quiet and listen. Our parents were consulted so that nothing would go wrong. We were to leave at 5 a.m. on the last Friday of the school year. The bus would not wait; if we were not there on time, they would leave without us.

It was going to be the most exciting trip that many of us had ever had, since most of us had never been past Topeka — if we had made it that far. Our teacher, Mr. Newberry, and the principal, enthusiastically detailed our itinerary: We would go to the Nelson-Atkins Museum of Art in the morning, Swope Park Zoo where we would eat our lunches, and from there to the Kansas City Stockyards. It would take all day, so we had to keep to our schedule.

It is, in retrospect, amazing that it was considered possible to do all those things in one day, along with the trip to and from Manhattan on two-lane U.S. 24, whose traffic slowed down for every town in its path and in a school bus that by state law couldn't go faster than 45 mph.

My mama was practically deaf even when she wore her hearing aid, so my greatest fear was that she wouldn't hear the alarm on the fateful morning. Actually the alarm may never have gone off, or so she said. All we knew was that the phone rang and rang until my sister heard it and answered. It was my teacher. It was now 5:30 a.m. And everyone was on the bus, but he just didn't have the heart to leave without me.

While I hastily got dressed, Mama rushed to prepare the sack lunch of roast beef sandwiches wrapped in wax paper, an apple, and peanut butter cookies, and with her housecoat inside out over her pajamas she drove me to the school in our black Chevy, where I boarded the bus to the cheers of my classmates. I still hadn't combed and braided my pigtails.

I don't remember everything about the rest of the day. At the Nelson-Atkins Museum, we were struck dumb by the grandeur of the Italian marble columns in the great center hall. We saw the diorama display of Navajo Indians weaving blankets. We also saw their baskets, beads, pottery and clothing made from the skins of animals that we had studied. We bought postcards with prints of paintings that we never saw.

The zoo was forgettable, lost in the subsequent horror of seeing the men club cows to death at the stockyards.

It was late when we pulled up in front of the school and stumbled out. It had been a most unusual and awesome day. Mama was waiting.

It was going to be the most exciting trip that many of us had ever had.

Baby elephant Dolly Dumbo on view at the Swope Park Zoo, in the 1940s.

175

Published on November 3, 1996

Truman and election day

By Authorene Phillips

*Harry S Truman
voting in 1954.*

*I*t was Election Day, 1962. My husband, Ed, and I were beginning teachers, and we arrived early to start our day at Palmer Junior High School in Independence.

Palmer is close to former President Harry S Truman's home. And many days as we drove to work, we exchanged waves with Truman, walking briskly on his way to work at the nearby Truman Library.

To be sure, we had heard that Truman and his wife, Bess, always voted early. But we never expected what was about to happen that November morning nearly 34 years ago.

My husband parked our 1950 Chevy in front of a green Dodge across from the junior high school. I gathered up my books while he climbed out, opened the trunk, reached in to lift out a box of science notebooks he'd taken home to grade ... and stopped abruptly.

Coming down the steps of the Memorial Building were President and Mrs. Truman.

"Good mornings" were exchanged. Then the former president nodded toward the box of notebooks and joked, "Stuffing the ballot boxes, huh?"

Seeing our surprise, he added, "That would have been a good question in my day."

Bess Truman was in the car by that time.

Although I had grown up as a Kansas girl and had heard all the criticisms of this Democratic president, I knew I was in the presence of a great man and asked to shake his hand.

He complied with a smile — and a firm grip — making this an Election Day to remember.

We had heard that Truman and his wife, Bess, always voted early.

TWA's Sky Tourist Constellation flights carried as many as 81 passengers on its U.S. routes.

Published on July 1, 2001

TWA: glory days

By Reta Jo Mitchell

Many older air travelers remember how glamorous flying once was. And expensive.

Hearing that American Airlines planned to acquire the beleaguered Trans World Airlines was like deja vu for the TWA family. Wasn't our collective memory stuffed with downturns, layoffs, even other bankruptcies? Wasn't TWA like the fabulous phoenix, that legendary bird reborn again from its own ashes?

But sometimes even legends die.

In 1957 my husband, a Navy flight engineer, applied to both TWA and Pan American for a job. TWA's offer came first, then Pan Am's telegram caught up with us in Oklahoma. We had wanted Pan Am so we could remain in San Francisco, but we feared the tires wouldn't make it back to California. So Kansas City, here we came. And except for one short transfer and one long layoff, here we have remained.

Our out-of-town relatives loved spending hours on top of the old terminal building (at Downtown Airport) watching the Connies lift off. A special memory lingers from 1964, when our 10-year-old Oklahoma nephew came up to see the KC Athletics play the Yankees. Late at night, we went to see the Yankees' plane arrive, and Johnny was thrilled when the great Yogi Berra autographed his catcher's mitt. Suddenly, though, our 3-year-old son, Russell, began to cry. He thought we'd come out to see his beloved Yogi Bear.

What memories we have of seeing the world on TWA! As long as we traveled light, our space-available passes and bright-red carry-ons took us everywhere. Who minded being bumped for a paying passenger when Paris lay just over the horizon?

Many older air travelers remember how glamorous flying once was. And expensive. In today's dollars, a 1955 Kansas City-to-Los Angeles round trip in tourist class cost $680. But the meals were good and the legroom better. Passengers flew dressed-up back then. But grandest of all were the berths on coast-to-coast flights with breakfast in bed.

Unforgettable were those months in 1975-76 when TWA employees voluntarily restored an old Northrup Alpha plane from TWA's past, then gave it to the Smithsonian.

So will TWA vanish altogether? No. Volunteer pilots, flight engineers, mechanics and flight attendants — active and retired — are transforming the Save-A-Connie Museum here into an impressive salute to airline history. It's now called the Airline History Museum at Kansas City.

For now, here's a test: You can always pick out a TWAer. They're the ones looking up when that beautiful 1049G Constellation roars overhead. They flew them. They fixed them. She is one of their dear old friends.

TWA stewardesses "break ground" for their new training center, when muddy conditions forced them inside.

Published on October 31, 1999

TWA: stewardess school

By Lucille Ardrey

It was a dream job, and young women flocked to Kansas City to be interviewed.

Back in the glory days of TWA, when the airline was based in Kansas City and building up its stewardess pool, it received 90,000 applications for 1,600 positions. It was a dream job, and young women flocked to Kansas City to be interviewed. My daughter, Kathy, was one of the lucky ones chosen to go to the training school.

The requirements were very strict in those days. The women had to be single and no taller than 5 feet, 4 inches; weight had to be maintained at a prescribed level. Their hair was short and could not touch the collar. A few young women with long, flowing locks couldn't bear to cut their hair off and left.

Kathy's class had 10 to 12 women in it. They lived on the Plaza in a beautiful 57-unit apartment complex and rode buses to and from their classes at the Jack Frye International Training Center.

The girls had a varied schedule. They learned about makeup in beauty classes. They served meals to one another in a mock airplane where they practiced. They learned to carve Chateaubriand on a cart in the aisle.

Early in their training, an emergency landing was simulated. The lights went out and the students had to activate the escape slides. Some of the stewardesses-in-training panicked, and they were through.

Before graduation, the women who remained had to take the dreaded "fright flight." This was a real plane ride during which the pilot did rolls and a nosedive and simulated decompression. Some of the young women had air sickness and were dismissed.

By this point the class had dwindled, and Kathy was the only one left who lived in the area. The students were not allowed to go home for the holidays, so we invited them to our house for Christmas dinner.

The first uniform Kathy wore after graduation was a powder-blue business suit with a pillbox hat. In 1968, TWA used paper uniforms that matched the colors of the plane interiors and loosely followed the style of the countries the planes flew to. A short-skirted gray dress with a serving wench's white apron was the uniform for England; a wraparound toga was the outfit for Italy.

It was after she had flown for a while that I was able to go on one of Kathy's flights on a pass. (How I miss those passes!) She had a turnaround flight to Los Angeles, and I went along in first class. We landed in L.A., stopped off at the airport, then reboarded and came back home. I've been on many flights since, but that one on TWA during its glory days is one I'll never forget.

Published on July 30, 2000

Union Station: the massacre

By Jeanette Brucker

Scene at the Union Station Massacre, in 1933.

When I graduated from high school in 1933, my parents sent me on a trip to visit my Aunt Rose in Mayfield, Ky. My dad was a telegraph operator for the Missouri Pacific Railroad, and I could ride on a pass. But none of the trips I ever made matched the drama of being present at the Kansas City Union Station Massacre on June 17, 1933.

I came from a small town west of Kansas City called Frankfort, Kan., and had to change trains at Union Station. I got off the train and went into the station to wait. Even though I had graduated and was feeling very adult, I also felt overwhelmed by the high ceiling and the big room.

I started talking to a railroader on the next bench; I thought railroaders were part of a brotherhood, sort of Dad's family, so I wasn't afraid of talking to him.

Suddenly, I saw two men dressed in black suits hurrying toward the doors that led to the tracks. I thought they were meeting someone coming off the train, but it was strange to see them rushing when everyone else was moving slowly in the summer heat.

The men disappeared through the doors, and I heard gunshots. People started rushing to the doors amid noise and confusion.

I got up to see what was happening, but the railroader called out:

"Jeanette, be careful! You come back here and sit right down. Don't go outside."

Women were screaming, and there were more shots. Police ran across the station. I stared thinking about Aunt Rose and how worried she would be when I wasn't on time. And then I realized Dad would get the news of the shooting over the telegraph and he'd be worried.

When things calmed down, someone came over and asked if I was Joe Ellis' girl from Frankfort, and I said I was. I guessed someone would telegraph Dad, and he'd telegraph the station in Kentucky and tell Aunt Rose. Finally, a porter walked me out to where the train was waiting. That was the brotherhood of the railroads. They looked out for one another's families, too.

I think I slept the rest of the way. In Mayfield, the newspapers and radio were full of the story. All the kids in town had heard of the Union Station Massacre and knew I'd been there. They mostly wanted to know if I'd seen anybody get killed. A neighbor boy took me to the movies, and we saw the newsreel of the shooting. "Oh, I was there!" I said, surprised.

So, for two weeks, I was a celebrity, and I got to tell my Kansas City story over and over. Nobody even got tired of hearing it.

I heard gunshots. People started rushing to the doors amid noise and confusion.

The Union Station waiting room in the 1940s.

Published on March 4, 2001

Union Station: stuck aboard

By Pat McGinley

Right: Last-minute traveler's needs at Union Station.

Below: The Union Station clock.

In May of 1945, I was 19 years old, and my best friend was my next-door neighbor, Mary. Mary's mother had been entertaining an out-of-town guest; the two had been partying heartily for two weeks.

When the day came for the guest, Helen, to leave for her home in Chicago, Mary got the job of getting her to Union Station and on the train. I went with her.

We were late, of course. Mary, who was driving, said: "I'll park the car while you get Helen to the gate. Meet you under the clock!"

The guard at the top of the stairs took one look — and smell, probably — at Helen and said, "You take her down the stairs and put her on the train." Because of the war effort — trains were packed with troops and equipment — the busy station didn't allow anyone without a ticket downstairs at the tracks. But the guard was making an exception for us.

Since there wasn't supposed to be anyone down there but actual passengers, the station had dispensed with the "All aboard!" call. The next thing I realized, when I looked up from settling Helen in her seat, the 6 p.m. express train was on its way to Chicago.

Even though I was hysterical, I found a conductor and hoped there'd be some place the train could stop before leaving the Kansas City area. In those ancient times, there was no communication with the outside world, and the wartime schedule of the railroads wasn't to be interrupted for a stupid girl who didn't have sense enough to get off the train on time.

There was no way to communicate to Mary waiting under the clock. My family would be frantic when they found I was missing.

The decision was finally made to drop me off in Marceline, Mo. (Marceline's main claim to fame is being the boyhood home of Walt Disney.) It was 2 1/2 hours away, the first station on the route that was open all night. A train would pick me up around 6 the following morning and get me back to Kansas City. By the time I returned, it would be 9 a.m.

In the meantime, back at Union Station, Mary's father, a Rotary friend of the stationmaster, had mounted a thorough search of the train yards and the station itself. When I arrived in Marceline, the stationmaster there called Kansas City. He told them what had happened and when I would be returning.

Although I feared that Mary and my family would be angry, I was welcomed lovingly. As I left the station, I turned, looked at the clock and promised that next time I wouldn't be 15 hours late.

Published on January 31, 1999

Vanguard Coffee House

By Tom Koob

The Vanguard Coffee House in the 1960s.

In the 1960s, Kansas City didn't really have a Greenwich Village or Haight District. But we did have the Vanguard. This coffeehouse was in a small storefront at 43rd and Main.

The neighborhood, which included the Art Institute, was considered to be somewhat bohemian. The Vanguard, complete with a black ceiling and cappuccino machine, was a unique place to hang out and sip coffee or other non-alcoholic beverages.

The best thing about this coffeehouse, though, was the music. Stan, the owner, provided a stage for some of the best local folk and blues musicians. It was considered quite cool to sit at a small table in the darkened atmosphere and listen to Danny Cox play the blues. Danny was a regular at the Vanguard, and has continued to perform in the Kansas City area.

My favorite act was Brewer & Shipley. Before their national fame, this duo often was featured on weekends at the Vanguard. Their fine harmony and excellent guitar work provided many enjoyable evenings. I remember a New Year's Eve show around 1970. It was a typical Kansas City New Year's Eve with snow and ice, but we made it to the Vanguard to see Brewer & Shipley and a new comedian. The comedian was Steve Martin. His show was "wild and crazy" long before he achieved national recognition.

I'm sure many other Kansas City artists got their start at the Vanguard and went on to successful careers. But music tastes change, and the Vanguard was too small for walls of amplifiers and mass audiences. I believe Stan went on to help open the Cowtown Ballroom. In the early 1970s, this venue featured many big-name rock acts.

The Vanguard provided a much more intimate place to appreciate music. In a time of change when music was almost constantly being redefined, this Kansas City coffeehouse was a nexus for folk and blues craftsmen and an appreciative audience of "bohemians."

The best thing about this coffeehouse, though, was the music.

Brewer & Shipley, famous for the song "One Toke Over the Line."

Published on April 25, 1998

Volker Park

By Danny Stevens Jr.

Volker Park in 1971.

It was the summer of 1969. I was 4 years old. My brother, Vince, was 3, my father, Danny Sr., was 23 and my mom, Nancy, was 20.

My parents worked long hours, and they didn't make much money. Raising two boys is expensive, and we spent many long nights at our grandma's house.

We lived on Elmwood Street. It was a colorful neighborhood that provided many memories, but the place I remember best is Volker Park.

When weekends rolled around, Mom continued to work. She did all she could to help the family. So Dad would take us boys to play at Volker Park.

The park was alive with people during nice summer weekends.

There was always something going on. We could play catch, throw a Frisbee, climb in the trees, roll in the grass or play in those grand fountains. On hot summer days there was nothing better than those fountains. Each weekend my brother and I looked forward to playing in the park with Dad. There were Frisbee tournaments to watch or somebody would be reading poetry aloud by the fountains. On breezy days the sky was filled with colorful kites.

There is one outing I will never forget. As we arrived in the park a rock 'n' roll band was setting up on the lawn. There were four men sitting on stools with a drummer behind them.

The drummer seemed to keep things rolling, though one of the guitarists with a full beard helped things flow. It was a free concert by a group no one had heard of.

The drummer and the bearded guitar player did most of the singing. The group drew the attention of everybody in the park. After each song, the crowd clapped appreciatively.

I remember the final song they sang that day. Everyone liked it. Lots of people danced. One of the verses went like this: "I'm a running down the road tryin' to loosen my load. I got seven women on my mind ..."

As Dad, Vince and I were leaving I heard one of the guys in the band say to the crowd: "Thank you all being so kind. The name of our band is the Eagles. We hope to make it big someday."

The park was alive with people during nice summer weekends. There was always something going on.

The Waldo streetcar stop in 1947.

Waldo

By Mary McKenna Trusler

I grew up in the Waldo area in a two-story brick house with the best yard on the block.

Each summer, as temperatures soar and my three children are abuzz with hot weather activities, my thoughts turn to simpler times — summer in the 1960s.

My brother, three sisters and I grew up in the Waldo area in a two-story brick house with the best yard on the block.

It was the best because of the crumbling concrete steps that descended a sloping terrace to the sidewalk. Best because of the streetlight out front. Best because all 19 neighbor kids congregated there to while away the lazy summer days.

Mayonnaise jars were transformed into houses for lightning bugs. Hopscotch patterns were etched on the sidewalk with whatever rock was suitable and handy.

Clothesline cord made fine jump ropes. Slugs that dared to invade our territory met an untimely demise, thanks to a spare handful of salt. And ice cubes proved a cure-all for whatever ailed us, be it thirst, hunger, heat or bee stings.

A shortage of baseball bats and gloves led to kickball, a team sport that involved kicking a ball and running bases. A lack of sports equipment never meant a lack of fun.

Occasionally — and only after extensive pleading — our mother allowed us to trek six blocks to the Little Store, a candy shop where penny candy really sold for 1 cent. We felt quite worldly on the return trip, each toting a miniature sack filled with jaw breakers, candy necklaces and the like. Only as a grown-up did I realize that the dime Mom gave each of us on those rare excursions took quite a bite out of the weekly budget.

As dusk deepened to dark, bedtime approached. Weary mothers, one by one, beckoned the neighborhood children home. After the last of our friends had departed up, down or across the street, my brother, sisters and I at last heeded our own mother's pleas to come inside. Another perfect summer day had ended.

"Bye, you guys! See you tomorrow!"

The West Bottoms in 1926, seen from Kersey Coates Drive.

Published on August 15, 1999

West Side

By Lois Counts McCain

We would climb up on the statue of Jim Pendergast and look out over the West Bottoms.

My family lived on the West Side, at 1628 Penn, between the years 1922 and 1934. Three of us attended Franklin Grade School and West Junior High. My older siblings attended Manual High. My favorite teacher was Miss Ella D. Jones in the sixth grade. My first experience of going to a Downtown movie and "eating out" at the Forum Cafeteria on Main Street was as her guest.

Kids were regular customers at Gould's store, where we bought candy, pencils and tablets. We played at Mulkey Square Park. We would climb up on the statue of Jim Pendergast and look out over the West Bottoms. To go swimming, we had to walk the long distance to Penn Valley Park. Every Friday night found us at the Summit Theatre at 17th and Summit to see cowboy shows and weekly serials. We saw many gangster movies with James Cagney. Tarzan was my favorite serial; Shirley Temple was my favorite star.

We bought our groceries at Louis Chenikoff's store. Louie and Rose were good to everyone. My two brothers worked there to help buy groceries. People bought groceries on credit. When we were ill, Mama took us to the Cabot Clinic. It cost 25 cents a visit, but if you could not afford that, it was free.

Big events in our lives included the fire department opening a hydrant and letting us play in the running water; the ice cream wagon or the hot tamale man and his cart coming by; the ice man giving us chips of ice; and hucksters selling fruits and vegetables from their wagons. There was a large mansion with a wrought-iron fence around it at 16th and Jefferson. The kids wondered who was rich enough to live there. It was rumored that gangsters did. They may have.

There were many gangsters living in our neighborhood.

To go all the way downtown was a treat for us. When Mama needed material to make a new apron she would take Frank and me with her. We would walk over to Broadway and up 12th Street past the Folly Theater (Mama always walked us on the opposite side of the street so we wouldn't see "those pictures of sinful women"), past the Muehlebach to Main Street, down past Kresge dime store and Harzfeld's to the next block. At Grant's dime store she got her 10-cents-a-yard material and five-cent bias tape. Frank and I got our treat: an ice cream sandwich. We spent all of a quarter on our outing, but that was a lot for one time. Money was scarce.

We would walk the 12 blocks back home with all of us happy and Mama anxious to get to work on her new apron.

Published on August 6, 1995

WHB radio

By Ernie Whitney

Count Basie and the Kansas City Seven in 1940.

*I*t was August 1938, and I was just starting my first job after college in an exciting new industry called radio.

Pioneer station WHB, with penthouse studios atop the Scarritt Building at Ninth Street and Grand Avenue, had given me a broom closet-sized office, a battered Underwood typewriter and an ultimatum to "write some radio advertising that will sell our sponsors' goods." All this for $17.50 a week, which in those days included Saturdays until 1 p.m.

Fortunately, in Kansas City in 1938, a person didn't need a lot of cash to have a good time. Nightclubs were everywhere. Coca-Cola cost 5 cents, beer was 10 cents, and nearly every tavern offered free shrimp on Friday nights.

Little did I realize that several people at WHB were destined to become famous. One such was the newscaster John Cameron Swayze. John's unusual voice and authoritative delivery brought him to the attention of NBC, and a few years later he was on his way to New York. Once in the Big Apple, Swayze soon switched over to an even newer medium called television.

Another famous person I got to know at WHB was Walter Cronkite, then a reporter for United Press. He was so determined to break into radio that whenever he wasn't chasing a fire for the wire service he was usually hanging around our studios. Some senior executives even thought he worked there!

Each afternoon at 3, WHB had an informal musical show featuring local talent singing popular songs. Seated at the studio organ for many of these shows was Bill Basie from Red Bank, N.J. He played piano at night at a local hot spot called the Reno Club but picked up what he called "walking around money" by playing on the radio. Today, of course, the world knows him as Count Basie.

Whenever a young man really wanted to impress a young lady, he invited her for dinner and dancing at some swank supper club that featured a famous dance orchestra. Playing at the Terrace Grill in the Hotel Muehlebach — and broadcasting three times daily on WHB — was the band of Ted Weems. It featured a young baritone from western Pennsylvania who, at least while in Kansas City, was fed up with his career.

On a visit to a 12th Street haberdashery, he told the salesman: "Singing with the dance orchestra is the pits. You travel all the time. You're never home." Then he declared that he was headed home for his hometown and his old job at the barbershop.

Fortunately, these plans never worked out. The ex-barber's name, you see, was Perry Como.

Little did I realize that several people at WHB were destined to become famous.

Whizzo the Clown

By Joe Morgan

Whizzo the Clown in 1968.

Back in the good old days when the kids were small and TV was in glorious black and white, Kansas City's answer to Buffalo Bob was Whizzo the Clown. With a live hour-long TV show at the prime noon hour, he had a good lock on the kindergarten and younger crowd. With his funny hat, bulbous nose and long shoes, he opened many a meat market. Whenever he appeared anywhere nearby, the kids dragged us along to see this latter-day Pied Piper.

Each TV show included about 20 local kids. He had his snappy banter and bag of tricks, but the kid interviews and marches — they all stomped behind him around the studio — were the highlights of the show. Also, the most unpredictable parts.

All the kids wanted to be on the show to talk and march with their hero. Finally my youngest daughter, Molly, who was about 6 at the time, and a neighborhood buddy got their call to make their show-biz debut.

My wife frantically worked on a special dress for Molly. The other kids were secretly envious, but old blase dad laughingly passed it off as nothing special. Except that I did take my portable TV and my lunch to work on the big day. With the TV handy and my constant babble about my little girl's debut on the stage, I suddenly gained a full house at the office as we all sat and awaited the big event.

Sweating through the commercials and the introductory chatter, I thought the kids would never appear. But then they were on in a nervous rush. As they marched around behind Whizzo with their balloons and pointed party hats I swelled with pride. "That's my kid there. No, the littlest one at the back that's always out of step."

After a few other maneuvers, the interviews were on. The kids sat on the great man's lap, and he asked questions geared to get funny answers only kids can come up with. I didn't envy him as he mostly ran into embarrassed and stammering silences.

And then Molly was on.

"I'm Molly," she said.

"You're Polly, what a funny name." he said. "Wanta cracker?"

"No, Molly, Molly."

He persisted. "Polly huh?" (Back at the office my friends sympathetically smiled at old dad as his kid got dissected on the tube.) Finally Molly retreated to her seat in frustrated tears.

I muttered under my breath as the hour wound down to the grand finale where Whizzo marched the kids out of the studio. Thinking perhaps to placate Molly, he leaned down, took her hand and said, "Here Polly, you march with me." That giant nose was just too much temptation for the kid. She threw a fast and mighty left hook that connected perfectly. Nose awry, amid great confusion, Whizzo somehow shuffled the children off, and the show was over.

Molly was, of course, the star of the show at our office, but we all agreed that it would perhaps be better for her to look to another field of work. Maybe bronco riding.

Years later I saw an article on Whizzo. He looked older, but his nose seemed completely restored. He was lucky he never ran into Molly's youngest, Megan. She has rearranged several noses in the family, and I'm afraid that large red target would have been just too much for her. POW!

Kansas City's answer to Buffalo Bob was Whizzo the Clown.

Wolferman's department store downtown on Walnut Street.

Published on February 14, 1999

Wolferman's

By Virginia Sandy McLaury

It was heaven. If I close my eyes today,
I can still see and taste it.

The recent closing of the Wolferman's plant in Lenexa brought back a lot of memories when I read about it.

My mother was an inveterate shopper who probably went shopping at least once a week. Now, shopping in those days meant riding the bus downtown from the east side of Kansas City to 11th and Grand and then shopping for the day. I don't remember liking to shop when I was young, but I always liked going because after we were through, we went to Wolferman's to eat. So I loved to go with her. It helped that she bought me something if I was along.

We shopped at Kline's mostly, sometimes Emery, Bird, Thayer, or Peck's (that was where the money traveled all around the store in a receptacle up around the ceiling to a cashier, who would make change and send it back to you) or Jones. Later on, we also shopped at Adler's.

But when Mom was finished, well, then we went to Wolferman's for a treat. I think the store was on Walnut Street between 11th and 12th. The first floor was a grocery department with a meat department and a butcher, fresh vegetables and a bakery — for the English muffins they were so famous for. But above that on a balcony, if I remember right, was a little eating area where you could get some meals or dessert.

I remember hamburgers served with some kind of pickle relish, English muffins that had been broiled just enough to brown the tips of the dough, and dessert, the best hot fudge sundaes I have ever eaten to this day. The sundaes were served in a sundae dish with the toppings on the side. The hot fudge came in a dull silver pitcher that you used yourself to pour over the ice cream. It was heaven. If I close my eyes today, I can still see and taste it.

Once in awhile, I would try something else, chocolate malts so thick you couldn't use a straw and huge chocolate sodas, but I always came back to the hot fudge sundae. You can see I loved chocolate then and still do.

I don't remember when Wolferman's downtown closed or when we stopped going downtown to shop, but it must have been when the shopping centers were built. But that's another story. And today, my mind is full of yesterday and hot fudge sundaes.

Grrrtrude Gorilla, Sam Panda, Dan'l Coon and friends at Worlds of Fun in 1977.

Published on May 28, 2000

Worlds of Fun

By Rhonda Wheeler Stock

It's been a rite of passage for kids north of the river for more than a quarter of a century. The Christmas decorations come down, a new year begins and fresh-faced 16-year-olds begin pounding the doors of this Northland institution. Soon these hopeful souls will be ushered into the adult world of W-4s and tax exemptions as they apply for their first "real" jobs. The pay is low and the hours are odd, but what other position offers free admission to an amusement park all summer long?

Ladies and gentlemen, welcome to Worlds of Fun.

As a high school student in the late 1970s, I served my time at WOF along with many of my friends. For two summers I worked a cash register in Europa's hat shop, stocked shelves at the Orient's gift shop and weighed candy in the Americana section. For a time I was Americana's flower girl. Perched in the breezeway between a couple of shops, I fashioned giant flowers with dowel rods, rubber bands, and huge sheets of tissue paper. It was actually pretty fun, and I especially enjoyed customizing a flower to someone's school colors.

The hat shop was fun, too, because we learned to use the embroidery machine. The machine was a bit like an old-fashioned treadle sewing machine, but with a handle underneath that allowed you to move the needle and form letters. It wasn't difficult once you got the hang of it, but passers-by were impressed. Once, an Israeli tourist asked us to do his name in Hebrew. He drew the letters on paper and one of the girls carefully followed the pattern. She must have done well because he was pleased with the results.

Probably the worst part of the job was the costumes. At the end of each shift we were required to exchange the dirty uniform for a fresh one from the wardrobe department. If they happened to be out of your size, you were stuck with shorts that gave you an eight-hour wedgie or a shirt that could wrap around you twice and still leave room for the entire cast from the Moulin Rouge. The outfits from Europa were a particular nuisance when you had to make a fast dash to the bathroom — it took a lot of time to unfasten the embroidered suspenders, unlace the shorts, then reverse the process when you were done.

My stints at WOF left me with a farmer's tan, an expanded — and colorful — vocabulary and a greater knowledge of human sexuality. (I've been married 17 years and I still haven't figured out some of the graffiti in the employees' bathroom.) The experience also gave me three important rules to live by. One, pity the poor guy who cleans up-chuck from hot asphalt when the temperature is 102 degrees and the humidity is 87 percent. Two, think twice when someone asks, "Why don't you do the test ride for the Schussboomer this morning?" And three, when you find a pair of shorts that fit, don't turn 'em in. Ever.

Wyandotte High School fire

By George Kvaternik

Wyandotte High School, the day after the fire, in 1934.

Published on December 13, 1998

It was a sad summer night in the 1930s when we learned that our high school was on fire. Wyandotte High School in downtown Kansas City, Kan., had been a home and a landmark for many a year, and it was a sad spectacle indeed to see it roaring in flames.

Although radio and telephone were the only means of communication, word spread quickly.

Groups of students huddled, sobbing; other pairs hugged tightly as if to squeeze out the pain of what they were seeing. An occasional crude joke was made in a hollow voice as were the grunts that followed, all feeling terribly out of place.

As we watched, there was a gasp and a cry as each section fell into its place in the flames. We remembered our favorite classroom and our favorite friends we met there, and our favorite teachers, too — some odd, some funny, but most dedicated to providing us with the knowledge necessary to succeed in the outside world.

Good moral attitudes were not forced on us; rather, we seemed to accept them as things to believe in. I do not remember hearing the word "dropout." We heard of only one girl getting pregnant, for which she was promptly expelled. Even the poorest students dressed neatly and cleanly. There were no guns, no knives, no gangs, no drugs, no weirdos hiding their insecurity behind ghoulish frill.

The only fear we had as we walked down the halls was the next class we had not properly prepared for. Of course, there was always the chance we would get a smile from the pretty girl we hoped someday to get up the nerve to meet!

As the flames grew higher, the students grew quieter, realizing that there never again would be a grand old Wyandotte High School, a place that asked for nothing but gave to each hope, desire, faith and warmth.

I wonder how many remember this fine old place. We need to praise and thank those who built and graced such a place, maybe hoping that someday such dreamers will return. Some of us who saw the smoldering ruins the next day hoped the school did not go out with a whimper but rather in a blaze of glory.

As we watched, there was a gasp and a cry as each section fell into its place in the flames.

Photo credits

Page 4

Herefords in the American Royal arena, circa 1935. Photo courtesy: Special Collections, Kansas City Public Library, Kansas City, Missouri.

Pages 6-7

Watching the American Royal Parade. Photo courtesy: Jackson County Historical Society Archives.

Horse riders at the American Royal Parade. Photo courtesy: Jackson County Historical Society Archives.

Page 8

Looking north on Baltimore Avenue at 11th Street, circa 1950s. KC Star Archives.

Page 10

Volker Fountain in 1966. KC Star Archives.

Pages 12-13

Thomas Hart Benton in 1941. The Kansas City Star photo archives

Benton's portrait of Lincoln at Lincoln University, in Jefferson City; photo taken in 1955. KC Star Archives.

Page 14

Children with their bicycles. Sign in spokes reads: Join Wards Bike Parade, Win a Prize. Photo courtesy: Special Collections, Kansas City Public Library, Kansas City, Missouri.

Page 16

Fans watch a Kansas City Blues game in 1948 at Blues Stadium. KC Star Archives.

Pages 18-19

Inside the old Board of Trade in 1927. Anderson Photo Co.

Baltimore Avenue, looking north to the old Board of Trade Building, in 1938. KC Star Archives.

Page 20

The Boulevard Drive-In in 1955. KC Star Archives.

Pages 22-23

Jack Dempsey, circa 1930s. KC Star Archives.

Gene Tunney in 1927. Harris & Ewing.

Page 24

Bob and Ernie Arfsten, current and past

owner of Brookside's the Dime Store, in 1979. KC Star Archives.

Page 26

Illustration by Lisa Morgan.

Pages 28-29

Chiefs quarteback Len Dawson. KC Star Archives.

Tommy Brooker in 1969. KC Star Archives.

Lamar Hunt in 1967. KC Star Archives.

Page 30

Petticoat Lane at Christmastime, circa 1910-1930. Looking east along 11th from Main. Photo courtesy: Special Collections, Kansas City Public Library, Kansas City, Missouri.

Pages 32-33

Christmas parade in downtown Kansas City. KC Star Archives.

Talking to Santa. KC Star Archives.

Pages 34-35

Enjoying the downtown Christmas windows in 1971. KC Star Archives.

Gold crowns decorate downtown intersections in 1971. Photo shows 11th and Main. KC Star Archives.

Page 36

After the Convention Hall fire, 1900. KC Star Archives.

Page 38

Singing cowboy Gene Autry. American Movie Classics photo.

Page 40

Delivery wagon in Independence in the 1920s. Photo courtesy: Jackson County Historical Society Archives.

Page 42

Joltin' Joe DiMaggio. UPI/Bettman HBO photo.

Page 44

Dixon Hotel in 1923, at 12th and Baltimore. KC Star Archives.

Page 46

About 500 people attended the premiere of the Terrace Grill at the Muehlebach Hotel in 1936. KC Star Archives.

Page 48

Twelfth Street in the early 1940s. KC Star Archives.

Pages 50-51

The Kresge dime store lunch counter, in 1951. KC Star Archives.

Harzfeld's department store at 11th and Main, in 1951. KC Star Archives.

Page 52

Baby chicks used to come in pastel colors at Eastertime. Photo circa 1967. KC Star Archives.

Page 54

The Manor Bread wagon, making deliveries in 1941. KC Star Archives.

Page 56

Fairyland Park in the 1940s. Photo courtesy: Wilborn and Associates, Kansas City, Missouri.

Page 58

Lined up to eat at the Forum Cafeteria, in the 1940s. Photo courtesy: Wilborn and Associates, Kansas City, Missouri.

Pages 60-61

Lining up for a free Christmas Dinner at St. Christopher's Inn in 1949. KC Star Archives.

Page 62

Hats, 1956, 1956, 1956, 1961, 1963. KC Star Archives.

Page 64

Horace Mann Elementary, circa 1930s. KC Star Archives.

Page 66

Illustration by Lisa Morgan.

Page 68

Independence, West Lexington Street on the south side of the courthouse square. KC Star Archives.

Page 70

The Indian Head Root Beer Stand once near 36th and State in Kansas City, Kan. Photo courtesy of the Wyandotte County Historical Society.

Page 72

Illustration by Lisa Morgan.

Page 74

The Kansas City Power & Light Building, looking up Baltimore, circa 1920-1930. Photo courtesy: Wilborn and Associates, Kansas City, Missouri.

Page 76

The Katz Drug store at Eighth and Grand, in 1923. KC Star Archives.

Pages 78-79

Shopping at the Kresge dime store, 1951. KC Star Archives.

The Kresge dime store at 12th and Main,

in 1951. KC Star Archives.

Page 80

Mrs. El Mehdi Ben Aboud, the wife of the Moroccan ambassador, cuts the cake during Liberty Memorial rededication ceremonies in 1961, while Harry S Truman looks on. KC Star Archives.

Pages 82-83

Loew's Midland Theatre, in 1927. KC Star Archives.

Clark Gable and Vivien Leigh wowed moviegoers in Gone With the Wind. KC Star Archives.

Page 84

Loose Park in 1945. KC Star Archives.

Page 86

Flamboyant Gorgeous George (Wagner) grew his hair long, dyed it blond, then pinned it back with gold-plated bobby pins during his heyday, 1940s to the early 1960s. Courtesy Bob Geigel.

Page 88

Metcalf South Shopping Mall in 1967. KC Star Archives.

Page 90

Janie Fopeano, the Milgram's lady. KC Star Archives.

Page 92

Hemlines inching up in 1969. KC Star Archives.

Page 94

Minnesota Avenue in 1951. KC Star Archives.

Page 96

The Royal Theater at 1022-24 Main. KC Star Archives.

Pages 98-99

The cast of Ice Capades in 1941. KC Star Archives.

Pages 100-101

Municipal Stadium in 1960. KC Star Archives.

The pinch-hit single by Don Bollweg that broke open the A's initial game in the sixth inning, in Municipal Stadium, in April 1955. KC Star Archives.

Pages 102-103

Children watching a performance in Music Hall, circa 1950. Special Collections, Kansas City Public Library, Kansas City, Missouri.